THE DYNAMICS OF
SOCIAL PRACTICE

SAGE has been part of the global academic community since 1965, supporting high quality research and learning that transforms society and our understanding of individuals, groups and cultures. SAGE is the independent, innovative, natural home for authors, editors and societies who share our commitment and passion for the social sciences.

Find out more at: **www.sagepublications.com**

THE DYNAMICS OF
SOCIAL PRACTICE

EVERYDAY LIFE AND HOW IT CHANGES

ELIZABETH SHOVE, MIKA PANTZAR & MATT WATSON

Los Angeles | London | New Delhi
Singapore | Washington DC

© Elizabeth Shove, Mika Pantzar & Matt Watson 2012

First published 2012
Reprinted 2012

SAGE Publications Ltd
1 Oliver's Yard
55 City Road
London EC1Y 1SP

SAGE Publications Inc.
2455 Teller Road
Thousand Oaks, California 91320

SAGE Publications India Pvt Ltd
B 1/I 1 Mohan Cooperative Industrial Area
Mathura Road, Post Bag 7
New Delhi 110 044

SAGE Publications Asia-Pacific Pte Ltd
3 Church Street
#10-04 Samsung Hub
Singapore 049483

Library of Congress Control Number: 2011931976

British Library Cataloguing in Publication data

A catalogue record for this book is available from the British Library

ISBN 978-0-85702-042-0
ISBN 978-0-85702-043-7 (pbk)

FSC
www.fsc.org
MIX
Paper from
responsible sources
FSC® C013604

Typeset by C&M Digitals (P) Ltd, Chennai, India
Printed and bound by CPI Group (UK) Ltd, Croydon, CR0 4YY
Printed on paper from sustainable resources

CONTENTS

LIST OF FIGURES AND TABLE

Figures

Table

ABOUT THE AUTHORS

Elizabeth Shove is Professor of Sociology at Lancaster University. She has written widely on theories of practice, technology, consumption, environment and everyday life. Elizabeth held an ESRC climate change leadership fellowship, 'Transitions in Practice: Climate Change and Everyday Life' (2008–2012), and is currently part of the ESRC funded Sustainable Practices Research Group. Recent books include *Time, Consumption and Everyday Life: Practice, materiality and culture* (Berg, 2009), *The Design of Everyday Life* (Berg, 2007) and *Comfort, Cleanliness and Convenience: The social organization of normality* (Berg, 2003).

Mika Pantzar is Research Professor at the National Consumer Research Centre, Helsinki. Mika has published articles in consumer research, design and technology studies, the rhetoric of economic policy, future studies and systems research and has written two books in Finnish: *Future Home: Inventing needs for domestic appliances* (Otava, 2000) and *Domestication of Technology: From science of consumption to art of consumption* (Tammi, 1996). His current research interests focus on the economics of sport, health and wellbeing.

Matt Watson is Lecturer in Human Geography at the University of Sheffield. In addressing empirical themes including consumption, waste and mobility, his work engages with a range of literatures including theorizations of practice and everyday life, of science and technology and of the structures and processes of governing. He is co-author, with Elizabeth Shove, Martin Hand and Jack Ingram, of *The Design of Everyday Life* (Berg, 2007).

ACKNOWLEDGEMENTS

Ideas developed in *The Dynamics of Social Practice* have circulated through seminars, conferences and working parties and have been shaped by many people along the way. Thanks to all and especially to Elizabeth's supervisory team at Lancaster – Allison Hui, David McBride, Julien McHardy and Nicola Spurling – and to Mikko Jalas who provided valuable input from Helsinki.

Mika Pantzar acknowledges support from the Finnish Academy for a research fellowship (2008–2011) Grant No. 118880.

This book would not exist without the UK's Economic and Social Research Council which funded Elizabeth Shove's Climate Change Leadership Fellowship, 'Transitions in Practice: Climate Change and Everyday Life', RES 066 27 0015.

THE DYNAMICS OF SOCIAL PRACTICE

How do societies change? Why do they stay so much the same? Within the social sciences, contrasting theoretical traditions have grown up around these enduring concerns. The problem of understanding novelty and persistence is surely not new, but it is one to which this book brings a fresh approach. It does so by developing a series of concepts with which to capture the dynamic aspects of *social practice*.

Our opening contention is that theories of practice have as yet untapped potential for understanding change. Realizing their potential depends on developing a means of systematically exploring processes of transformation and stability within social practices and between them. This is the task to which most of the following chapters are devoted. Whilst this is an important exercise in its own right, it is of more than academic concern.

In showing how practices change and stay the same we hope to realize another also latent promise, which is for social theory to make a difference. We do not offer instant solutions but we contend that our analysis is of value in responding to complex challenges like those of climate change and obesity, and in addressing persistent patterns of inequality. Theories of practice have yet to make much impact on public policy but it seems obvious that if 'the source of changed behaviour lies in the development of practices' (Warde, 2005: 140), understanding their emergence, persistence and disappearance is of the essence. It also seems obvious that the reproduction and transformation of social practices has implications for patterns of consumption and for institutions and infra-structures associated with them. In the final chapter we argue that pol-icy initiatives to promote more sustainable ways of life could and should be rooted in an understanding of the elements of which practices and systems of practice are formed, and of the connective tissue that holds them together.

The theoretical and practical significance of comprehending social change and stability is clear enough, but why do we need yet another book? What more is there to add to the many methods and perspectives already on offer? Detailed answers to these questions are woven through the chapters that follow, but the next few paragraphs give a sense of the position from which we begin, the resources on which we draw and the contribution we make to the project of understanding and analysing the dynamics of social practice.

For us, as for everyone else, methods of conceptualizing change reflect prior understandings of the relation between agency and structure. The idea that new social arrangements result from an accumulation of mil-lions of individual decisions about how best to act is enormously influ-ential in everyday discourse, in contemporary policy-making and in certain areas of social science. This idea, which carries with it multiple assumptions about human agency and choice, resonates with common sense theories as to why people do what they do. It also fits comfortably with the notion that behaviours are driven by beliefs and values and that lifestyles and tastes are expressions of personal choice. Although now so pervasive as to seem natural, interpretations of this kind belong within a specific tradition that is grounded in the utilitarianism of Bentham and Mill, and that runs consistently through to contemporary versions of rational choice theory. This is a tradition in which action is, in essence, explained by the pursuit of individual interests. While we recognize the popularity of this position and its importance in legitimizing efforts to induce change, for example, by educating people about the consequences of their actions or by modifying economic costs and benefits through taxes or incentives, this is not a position we share. Nor do we go along with the view that change is an outcome of external forces, technological innovation or social structure, somehow bearing down on the detail of daily life. Instead, when it comes to matters of agency and structure, our response is to side with Giddens (1984).

Giddens' structuration theory revolves around the conclusion that human activity, and the social structures which shape it are recursively related. That is, activities are shaped and enabled by structures of rules and meanings, and these structures are, at the same time, reproduced in the flow of human action. This flow is neither the conscious, voluntary purpose of human actors, nor the determining force of given social structures. While people can discursively account for their actions, often framing them in terms of conscious purposes and intentions, Giddens emphasizes that the greater part of the processes at stake do not lie within the realm of discursive consciousness. The capability to 'go on' through the flow of largely routinized social life depends on forms of practical knowledge, guided by structural features – rules and resources – of the social systems which shape daily conduct. In Giddens' words, it is through practices that the 'constitution of agents and structures are not two independently given sets of phenomena, a dualism, but represent a duality' (1984: 25). He consequently claims that

> the basic domain of study of the social sciences, according to the theory of structuration, is neither the experience of the individual actor, nor the existence of any form of social totality, but social practices ordered across space and time.
>
> (Giddens, 1984: 2)

In 1984, Giddens provided what was then, and perhaps is still, the clearest account of how theories of practice might transcend the dualisms of structure and agency, determination and voluntarism. By implication such theories should also provide a means of explaining processes of change without prioritizing human agency and choice, and of conceptualizing stability without treating it as an outcome of given structures. Sure enough, Giddens makes the point that 'the day to day activity of social actors draws upon and reproduces structural features of wider social systems' (1984: 24). Statements of this kind are entirely plausible, but in emphasizing societal *reproduction*, and in being framed at such a general level, they leave many questions hanging. Of these the most important have to do with exactly how practices emerge, evolve and disappear.

   In tackling these questions head on this book takes up the challenge of developing and articulating methods of understanding social order, stability and change in terms that are required and informed by theories of practice. Although this is a complicated task, it is one we approach with the help of a relatively simple conceptual framework assembled from ideas and strands of thought gathered from a range of disciplines and traditions. There is no shortage of writing about practice, and as such no need to start from scratch. In the remainder of this chapter we outline the theoretical foundations on which we build and introduce some of the materials we use.

INTRODUCING THEORIES OF PRACTICE

Theories of practice have roots stretching at least as far back as Wittgenstein and Heidegger. Whilst Wittgenstein does not write directly about 'practices', his work conveys many of the key features of theories of practice. For Schatzki (1996), Wittgenstein's location of intelligibility and understanding, not within discrete human minds but in the flow of praxis, and his articulation of how intelligibility and understanding structure of human action and the social realm provides a basis for a theorization of practices which recognizes that 'both social order and individuality ... result from practices' (1996: 13). Heidegger, in *Being and Time* (1962), identifies praxis, as much as language, as a source of meaning. His account of *Dasein* and its relation to human activity and to equipment resonates with the ontological grounding of theories of practice, again emphasizing that human action is always already in the world. There are points of connection between some of these ideas and earlier contributions from pragmatists like James and Dewey. These include the importance accorded to embodied skills and know-how and the contention that experience is best understood not as an outcome of events and intentional actions, but as an ongoing process or flow in which habits and routines are continually challenged and transformed. Despite differences of origin and emphasis, these philosophical precursors are alike in suggesting that practices are not simply points of passage between human subjects and social structure. Rather, practice is positioned centre stage.

From these early twentieth-century origins, somewhat more integrated accounts emerged in the 1970s and into the 1980s. Charles Taylor employed the idea of practice as a means to contest behaviourism, again locating practices as a primary unit of analysis,

> meanings and norms implicit in [...] practices are not just in the minds of the actors but are out there in the practices themselves, practices which cannot be conceived as a set of individual actions, but which are essentially modes of social relations, of mutual action.

> (Taylor, 1971: 27)

Meanwhile, in the social sciences, Bourdieu's work is more widely known. Despite titles like *Outline of a Theory of Practice* (1977) or *The Logic of Practice* (1990), Bourdieu did not develop a consistent theory of practice over his works. Within his writings, practices are more generally seen as a means of approaching his more central concern: that of theorizing *habitus* – a concept which in Bourdieu's hands embodies aspects of practical consciousness and of norms and rules of conduct, aspects that other theorists take to be part of practices themselves. Here it is habitus and practices which are in recursive relation, such that habitus is 'constituted in practice and is always oriented towards practical functions' (1990: 52). Nevertheless, Bourdieu was influential in bringing concepts of practice into the social theoretical debates of the 1980s, doing so at a time when these ideas resonated with other work, including that of Foucault.

Through these routes, theories of practice entered the vocabulary of social scientific enquiry. Although notions of practice figure in different strands of social science through the 1980s and 1990s, they gained fresh theoretical impetus towards the close of the twentieth century, primarily through the work of philosopher Theodore Schatzki. His exposition of a Wittgensteinian theory of practice (Schatzki, 1996) helped bring practices back into the firmament of ideas as the influence of the linguistic turn in social theory began to fade. In retrospect, *The Practice Turn in Contemporary Theory* (Schatzki et al., 2001) did not define a neat manoeuvre in social theory, but it did mark the start of what has become a diffuse movement, the shape and extent of which remains to be seen.

The essays collected in *The Practice Turn in Contemporary Theory* demonstrated a continuing variety of theoretical positions gathering under the practice banner. In 2002, cultural sociologist Andreas Reckwitz sought to make sense of this diversity and in so doing provided a cogent summary of key features common to the most prominent approaches, using this as a platform from which to characterize an 'ideal type of practice theory' (Reckwitz, 2002: 244). Reckwitz positions practice theories in relation to other cultural theories, all of which 'highlight the significance of shared or collective symbolic structures of knowledge in order to grasp both action and social order' (246). He groups cultural theories into three types, each distinguished by where they locate the social. 'Culturalist mentalism' locates the social in the mind, in the heads of humans, this being where knowledge and meaning structures are taken to reside. For 'culturalist textualism' the social is situated not in the mind but 'in chains of signs, in symbols, discourse, communication ... or "texts"' (248). Finally, 'culturalist intersubjectivism ... locates the social in interactions' (249), most obviously through the intersubjectivity of ordinary speech acts. In contrast to these three alternatives, theories of practice are distinct in contending that the social is situated in practice.

What, then, is practice? For Reckwitz, it is 'a routinized type of behavior' (2002: 249). Taken in isolation, this phrase is potentially misleading in that it risks equating practices with the habits of individuals.

Such an interpretation would miss the point in that it would overlook the recursive character of practice. This becomes obvious as Reckwitz goes on to explain that a practice exists as a 'block' or 'a pattern which can be filled out by a multitude of single and often unique actions' (2002: 250). In this sense, a practice endures between and across specific moments of enactment (Shove et al., 2007). As Schatzki puts it, a practice is 'a temporally and spatially dispersed nexus of doings and sayings' (1996: 89).

Reckwitz takes these ideas one step further in suggesting that a practice, as a block or pattern, consists of interdependencies between diverse elements including 'forms of bodily activities, forms of mental activities, "things" and their use, a background knowledge in the form of understanding, know-how, states of emotion and motivational knowledge' (2002: 249). To give a practical illustration, skateboarding consists of a complex amalgam of skateboards and street spaces along with the bodily competencies required to ride the board and to use the affordances of the street to turn tricks; the rules and norms that define the practice of skateboarding; its meanings to practitioners and to outsiders including its partially oppositional character, and so on. As such skateboarding exists as a recognizable conjunction of *elements*, consequently figuring as an *entity* which can be spoken about and more importantly drawn upon as a set of resources when doing skateboarding.

At the same time, practices exist as *performances*. It is through performance, through the immediacy of doing, that the 'pattern' provided by the practice-as-an-entity is filled out and reproduced. It is only through successive moments of performance that the interdependencies between elements which constitute the practice as entity are sustained over time. Accordingly, skateboarding only exists and endures because of countless recurrent enactments, each reproducing the interdependencies of which the practice is comprised.

In this analysis, individuals feature as the *carriers* or hosts of a practice. This is a radical departure from more conventional approaches in which understandings, know-how, meanings and purposes are taken to be personal attributes. Reckwitz argues that it makes better sense to treat these not as the qualities of an individual but as 'elements and qualities of a practice in which the single individual participates' (2002:

250). By implication, the significance, purpose and skill of skateboarding are not simply contained within the heads or bodies of skateboard-
ers; rather these features constitute the practice of skateboarding, of
which the rider is merely a carrier.

Much of the literature referred to above takes practices to be enduring
entities reproduced through recurrent performance. There is nothing
inherently wrong with this interpretation, but something more is
required if we are to develop a convincing account of change and order
with practice at its heart. To give a simple example, skateboarding has
a short but turbulent history during which it has undergone multiple
transformations – starting when surfers added wheels to boards, moving
through skate parks and now on to more contemporary forms of street
skateboarding (Borden, 2001). With each transition, elements, including
the shape of the board, the details of know-how, the meanings and purposes of the practice and its characteristics – as entity and as performance – have been reconfigured. At a minimum, we need to find ways of
describing and analysing processes like these while also accounting for
more faithful, more consistent forms of reproduction.

In showing how practice theories might be developed to better
account for change we make extensive use of many of the ideas sketched
above. For example, the proposition that practices are composed of elements and the suggestion that people are usefully understood as the
carriers of practice figure prominently in our account. The analytic distinction between practice-as-performance and practice-as-entity also
proves useful, allowing us to show how novel combinations of competence, material and meaning are enacted and reproduced. Like the practitioners and everyday innovators about whom we write, we appropriate
ideas from here and there, making new connections between existing
arguments as required. In the next section we highlight some of the
other literatures from which we borrow.

MATERIALS AND RESOURCES

Reckwitz classifies theories of practice as cultural theories. While they
differ from other cultural theories in where they situate the social, they

are alike in how the realm of the social is defined and in what it includes. For the most part, theories of practice have focused on the significance of shared understandings, norms, meanings, practical consciousness and purposes, all of which count as classically 'social' phenomena.

More recently, other less obvious elements have entered the frame. Schatzki argues that 'understanding specific practices *always involves apprehending material configurations*' (Schatzki et al., 2001: 3). Reckwitz is even more explicit. Using a very ordinary example he makes the point that: 'in order to play football we need a ball and goals as indispensable "resources"' (2002: 252). A ball alone does not make the game – an idea of playing, people to play with and a measure of competence are also necessary, and questions remain about how material and other elements combine. A key feature of our own approach is the emphasis we place on the constitutive role of things and materials in everyday life. In short, we take seriously Latour's statement that arte-facts 'are not "reflecting" [society], as if the "reflected" society existed somewhere else and was made of some other stuff. They are in large part the stuff out of which socialness is made' (2000: 113). In this we redress a partial but significant gap, adding a material dimension to what are otherwise conventionally 'social' theories.

In the process, we make selective use of ideas developed within science and technology studies (STS), a field which has a number of intellectual traditions in common with practice theory, but in which the role of things and technologies is a major theme. There are several clear points of connection, including *The Mangle of Practice* (Pickering, 1995), in which Pickering contends that practices are constituted through the actions of material entities as well as of people. Preda develops similar arguments, suggesting that artefacts are 'processes and ... knots of socially sanctioned knowledge' (1999: 362) that 'bind human actors and participate in developing specific forms of social order – because they allow for common practices to develop, stabilize and structure time' (355). Bruno Latour, perhaps the most influential theorist within STS, also features in Reckwitz' list of key figures involved in developing theories of practice, but for many Latour's claim that artefacts have the capacity 'to construct, literally and not metaphorically, social order' (2000: 113) is a step too far. Schatzki

(2002: 71) directly contests this 'extension of the categories of actor and action to entities of all sorts' and is critical of proponents of actor network theory who 'contend that practices comprise the actions of various entities and not those of people alone' (71). In Schatzki's scheme, artefacts, materials and technologies are not literally part of practices but instead form 'arrangements' that are co-produced with practices but which are nonetheless distinct. This leads him to argue that although actor network theory attends to the 'arrangement' aspect of this equation, it fails to recognize that 'the practices that are tied to arrangements ... help constitute social phenomena' (Schatzki, 2010a: 135). This discussion and others like it are symptomatic of more profound differences in how practices, materials and actors are conceptualized and in what this means for the relation between them.

In picking our way through these debates we are broadly sympathetic to the view that agencies and competencies are distributed between things and people, and that social relations are 'congealed' in the hardware of daily life. However, we do not go along with the idea (common in STS) that materials constitute the sticky anchor weights of social action or that they should be treated as immutable and relatively incorruptible transporters of power and influence (Law, 1991). While actor network theory has been useful in challenging overly neutral interpretations of the part (or non-part) things play in structuring social action, it has also led to a potentially leaden view of stuff. More abstractly, actor network theory has inspired politically and philosophically intriguing debates about the relation between humans and the non-humans with whom they share their lives, but has ironically done so in ways that divert attention away from more ordinary questions about what these cyborg/hybrid entities are actually *doing*. In response, we suggest that aspects of human and non-human relations can be *better* understood when located in terms of a more encompassing, but suitably materialized, theory of practice. Other authors reach much the same conclusion, defining technologies as 'configurations that work' (Rip and Kemp, 1998) and observing that 'individual technologies add value only to the extent that they are assembled together into effective configurations' (Suchman et al., 1999: 399).

In developing these ideas we also take such effective configurations to be the primary objects of study. However, we do not concentrate exclusively on the context-specific processes involved in producing localized configurations of knowledge, meaning, materiality and action. Our approach consequently differs, in terms of theory and method, from those who undertake detailed ethnographies of situated practice (Suchman, 1984; Hutchins, 1993; Orlikowski, 2002). Since we are interested in the trajectories of practices-as-entities, as well as in the performances of which these are formed, we are interested in how the spatial and temporal reach of 'working configurations' is constituted and how it changes. For this we need to look beyond specific moments of integration.

It is on these terms that we engage with theories of innovation. In recent years, authors who write about consumption, design, organization and innovation have begun to explore the parts 'end-users' play as collaborators, experimenters and co-producers of innovation in product or systems design. This literature challenges representations of professional designers and inventors as the primary source of novelty and complicates simple distinctions between producers on the one hand, and consumers on the other. Having identified multiple forms of collaboration and sharing between end-users, Franke and Shah (2003) conclude that using is itself a creative and innovative process. In the cases they describe, practices of mountain biking and snowboarding have been challenged, extended and developed through and as a result of the energy and enthusiasm of devoted practitioners, in association with an array of producers. In understanding how these processes work out, we need to find ways of integrating concepts from innovation studies with theories of practice.

A second relevant observation, also made by Franke and Shah, is that innovation in practice is an ongoing and not a one-off process. Within innovation studies it is normal to distinguish between conditions and relationships involved in first making something new and those that characterize subsequent stages of development and diffusion. Practice theories of the type we develop make it possible to bridge this gap and analyse invention, innovation and innofusion in similar terms, and in terms that acknowledge the active and dynamic relation between producers *and* consumers in making new arrangements *and* in developing and sustaining them over time.

When used in this way, practice theory provides a means of uniting studies of innovation and consumption and of conceptualizing dynamic processes inherent both in business and in other realms of everyday life. Such an approach has a number of further implications. One is to suggest that product innovations do not constitute solutions to existing needs. In so far as desires, competencies and materials change as practices evolve, there are no technical innovations without innovations in practice. In other words, if new strategies and solutions in product or service development are to take hold, they have to become embedded in the details of daily life and through that the ordering of society (Shove et al., 2007).

Others have recognized the close coupling of technical innovation and the organization of the social, and in developing this theme we selectively exploit the work of those who have written about trajectories of sociotechnical change, and the co-evolution of sociotechnical regimes and landscapes (Kemp et al., 2001; Geels, 2004). What has become known as the 'multi-level' model of innovation suggests that new 'sociotechnical' arrangements develop in protected niches; that developments at this 'micro' level are shaped by and have consequences for the formation of 'meso' level regimes and that these in turn structure and are structured by 'macro' level landscapes (Rip and Kemp, 1998: 338). By implication, the move from niche to landscape is one in which linkages become progressively denser and paths ever more dependent. As a result, landscapes are harder to change, and change more slowly than either regimes or niches. These ideas have proven useful and influential and have engendered interest in the possibility that strategic intervention at the 'lower' level might set in train a cumulative sequence of events, resulting in a wholesale shift, for example, towards a more sustainable path of sociotechnical development (Elzen et al., 2004).

There are obvious parallels between this approach and the view that practices are more and less faithfully reproduced by those involved in actively making links, and that it is through the successive enactment of practices that social orders are sustained, stabilized and disturbed. While we agree that forms of path-dependence matter and that sociotechnical systems and complexes of practice are shaped by multiple dynamic processes, our analysis of the development and demise of 'configurations that work' differs in two key respects. First, the simultaneity of *doing* is important for an understanding how practices are formed and how they change. While there are always points of connection between one performance of a practice and the next, and while forms of path dependence are vital, we are interested in synchronic as well as diachronic relations. Moments of doing, when the elements of a practice come together, are moments when such elements are potentially reconfigured (or reconfigure each other) in ways that subtly, but sometimes significantly change all subsequent formulations. Second, we argue that stability is the emergent and always provisional outcome of successively faithful reproductions of practice. When compared with day-to-day processes of social reproduction, the 'multi-level' model of social change and stability seems too ordered and too layered. In the account we develop, stabilization is not an inevitable result of an increasing density of interdependent arrangements, rather, practices are provisionally stabilized when constitutive elements are consistently and persistently integrated through repeatedly similar performances.

These introductory remarks provide some justification for the project on which we are about to embark, and make some sense of the intellectual resources enlisted along the way. Throughout the book we use empirical examples to articulate and exemplify the steps and stages of the position we develop. It is important to be clear about the status of these cases. Not all have immediate import for the big problems facing society: many, like skateboarding, are chosen because they help illustrate the points we want to make. These points nonetheless combine in a manner that allows us to demonstrate the relevance of practice theory for understanding and analysing the multiple dynamics of everyday life, and hence for addressing the major policy challenges of our time.

SEQUENCE AND STRUCTURE

The next five chapters introduce and explain the core features of our approach one step at a time. In simple terms, they move from a discussion of elements and practices through to more complex questions about how practices relate to one another. At the same time, each chapter works with a slightly different unit of analysis. In combination these strategies allow us to address the problem of how practices change and how they stay the same from different angles. In the process we explore five related questions:

1 How do practices emerge, exist and die?

2 What are the elements of which practices are made?

3 How do practices recruit practitioners?

4 How do bundles and complexes of practice form, persist and disappear?

5 How are elements, practices and links between them generated, renewed and reproduced?

Towards the end of the book we draw the pieces of our analysis together and discuss the implications of our account for theories of practice, and for related issues of space, time and power. This discussion informs the final chapter in which we review the practical relevance and the policy implications of focusing on the dynamics of social practice, rather than 'behaviour change' narrowly defined.

    In detail, the chapters are organized as follows. Chapter 2, 'Making and breaking links', suggests that in doing things like driving, walking or cooking, people (as practitioners) actively combine the elements of which these practices are made. By elements we mean:

• *materials* – including things, technologies, tangible physical entities, and the stuff of which objects are made;

• *competences* – which encompasses skill, know-how and technique; and

• *meanings* – in which we include symbolic meanings, ideas and aspirations.

We go on to argue that practices emerge, persist, shift and disappear when *connections* between elements of these three types are made, sustained or broken. In putting forward such a reductive scheme we may well have fallen 'prey to the scientific urge to build simplifying, diagrammatic models of social life' (Schatzki, 2002: xii). In defence, we contend that this simple formulation is useful in that it provides us with a means of conceptualizing stability and change, and does so in a way that allows us to recognize the recursive relation between practice-as-performance and practice-as-entity.

We introduce these ideas by re-examining moments in the history of automobility, taking the practice of *driving* rather than the car itself as the central topic. This exercise demonstrates the value of treating innovation in practice as a process of linking new and existing elements. As well as revealing critical moments when 'proto-practices' emerge and become real, such a method keeps aspects of continuity and change constantly in view. In addition, it provides an important reminder of the fact that the history of car-driving is a history in which previously established technologies, competences and meanings disintegrate and crumble, and in which practices that were once normal disappear. In responding to our first question – How do practices emerge, exist and die? – Chapter 2, 'Making and breaking links', introduces further lines of enquiry – what are the elements involved, where do they come from, how do they travel and how do they change?

In Chapter 3, 'The life of elements', we seek answers to these questions. In order to do so we proceed as if elements can be separated out and somehow detached from the practices of which they are a part. This methodological strategy allows us to explore the properties and characteristics of the three types of elements about which we write. In showing how materials, meanings and competences endure and travel, we provide a means of understanding how practices are sustained between moments and sites of enactment. We consider the role of transportation in shaping the geographical range of technologies (such as cast-iron stoves) and of practices associated with them. We then discuss forms of codification, abstraction and reversal, all of which are important for how competences travel and for how knowledge is transmitted from one cohort of practitioners to another. Meanings do not diffuse in quite the same way. In thinking about the processes involved we show how concepts of 'freshness' have been successively attached to the air, to the

laundry and to sensations of bodily cleanliness. By implication, meanings move and spread between practices by means of association and
classification.

Towards the end of this chapter we reflect on the emergence, persistence and disappearance of these three types of elements and on the
potential for accumulating and storing materials, meanings and forms
of competence. In addressing these themes, Chapter 3 explores the lives
of elements to which practitioners must have access if practices are to be
performed.

Chapter 4, 'Recruitment, defection and reproduction', addresses our
third question: How do practices recruit practitioners? It is more common to ask how people become committed to what they do, but in turning this question around we consider the consequences of broader
patterns of recruitment and defection for the reproduction of practices
across space and time. Again we explore the topic from different angles.
Studies of social networks and communities of practice underline the
importance of social ties between people for recruitment to new practices. Where practices are more established, and where they are inscribed
in existing infrastructures, routes of recruitment differ. In theory, patterns
of recruitment and defection are intimately related: as some practices
expand, so others contract. Yet the processes involved are not exactly the
same. We consider the brief but hectic life of fads such as hula-hooping,
using this and other examples to identify different narratives of abandon-
ment and decline. How did hula-hooping capture and then lose huge
numbers of recruits over a relatively short time? Was it because the practice was of little symbolic significance, was it because it failed to provide
much by way of intrinsic reward or because it never became enmeshed
in any more extensive practice complex? Somewhat different arguments
are needed to explain the longer, slower decline of commuter cycling, this
being a deeply embedded practice dislodged and displaced by an emerging
system of automobility. In the end, the purpose of this chapter is to show
how patterns of recruitment and defection play out over time and to
show what this means for the reproduction of some but not other practices, and hence for the character and structure of daily life.

Our discussion of recruitment and defection touches on broader questions about how practices relate to each other, and how such relations

matter for stability and change. This sets the scene for Chapter 5, 'Connections between practices', in which we address our fourth question: How do bundles and complexes of practice form, persist and disappear? As elements link to form practices, so practices connect to form regular patterns, some only loosely associated, others more tightly bound. For example, driving can be understood as a single practice or as a seamless integration of steering, checking the mirror, navigating and so on. By comparison, connections between the diverse practices that constitute what people take to be a particular 'lifestyle' are more open and more diffuse. In describing these differences we distinguish between *bundles* of practices, loose-knit patterns based on co-location and co-existence, and *complexes*, representing stickier and more integrated arrangements including co-dependent forms of sequence and synchronization. We go on to explore the bases of such connections and in so doing consider the manner in which practices compete and collaborate with each other. We argue that the emergent character of relations between practices has consequences for the individual practices of which bundles and complexes are formed, for the elements which comprise those practices and for shared temporal rhythms.

In Chapter 6, 'Circuits of reproduction', we tackle our fifth question: How are elements, practices and links between them generated, renewed and reproduced? Having underlined the point that practices emerge and are sustained through successive performances, we consider the 'circuits of reproduction' through which one performance relates to the next and identify forms of cross-referencing through which practices shape each other. We examine different forms of feedback related to the reproduction of practices-as-performances and to the unfolding careers of practices-as-entities. In discussing the relation between one enactment of a practice and the next, we write about how heart rate monitors shape future performances of fitness practices like running or cycling. Somewhat different types of 'monitoring' are involved in representing and reproducing the careers of practices-as-entities. In explaining how this works we discuss the emergence and development of snowboarding, this being a practice that has a short but rather well documented career.

We know that co-existing practices shape each other, but how does this actually happen? Clocks, watches and more recent technologies of mobile communication make a difference to the ways in which practices connect in the organization of daily life. Cross-referencing, by which we mean synchronous feedback between practices, is important for the coordination and scheduling of events. It is also important for the formation of more extensive bundles and complexes of practice and for how such conjunctions are reproduced. In figuring out how practices converge and how they connect as entities, we consider the emergence of obesity and its definition as a social problem that brings different aspects of daily life (eating, exercise) together by means of calculation, quantification and moral concern. In bringing this chapter to a close we reflect on the possibility that the forms of feedback we have discussed together constitute a more complex circuitry, the details of which are important for understanding how the fabric of society is sustained and how it changes.

Chapter 7, 'Representing the dynamics of social practice', reviews the key features of the argument built through Chapters 1 to 6 and summarizes the contribution we have made to the project of understanding how social practices change and how they stay the same. We go on to discuss the implications of our approach for conceptualizations of time and space. The proposition that time and space emerge from the flow of practices brings questions of distribution and equity to the fore. In touching on these themes we introduce some of the practical, political questions addressed in Chapter 8.

Chapter 8, 'Promoting transitions in practice', confronts the most challenging question we are likely to face: Is our analysis of the dynamics of social practice of any practical use? What difference does it makes if we take *practices* rather than individuals to be the unit of analysis and the target of policy intervention? In addressing this question we begin by articulating the social-theoretical foundation of strategies designed to promote behaviour change in relation to policy challenges like those of climate change and health. It does not take long to establish that most such programmes depend on viewing behaviour as a matter of individual choice, typically based upon personal attitudes but sometimes influenced by 'driving' factors, including social norms, habit and more rational considerations of price. This conceptualization of action overlooks the extent to which the details of daily life are anchored in and constitutive of the changing contours of social practice.

In keeping with the position developed in the rest of the book we argue that policy makers need to intervene in the dynamics of practice if they are to have any chance of promoting healthier, more sustainable ways of life. Patterns of stability and change are not controlled by any one actor alone, but policy makers often have a hand in influencing the range of elements in circulation, the ways in which practices relate to each other and the careers and trajectories of practices and those who carry them. The prospect of developing an explicitly practice-oriented approach to public policy is decidedly exciting, but we are the first to recognize that this depends on provoking and engendering a transition in dominant paradigms and in equally dominant ways of conceptualizing social change. Our ultimate aim is to shove debate in this direction.

2

MAKING AND BREAKING LINKS

We begin our analysis of the dynamics of social practice with two deceptively simple propositions. The first is that social practices consist of elements that are integrated when practices are enacted. The second is that practices emerge, persist and disappear as links between their defining elements are made and broken.

The contention that people are routinely engaged in making and breaking links of one kind or another is not particularly controversial. John Law writes about 'heterogenous engineers' (1987), who assemble 'bits and pieces from the social, the technical, the conceptual and the textual' so as to make sets of equally heterogeneous 'products' including scientific products, along with institutions, organizations, computing systems, economies and technologies (1992). And in anthropology, Appadurai's (1986: 18) analysis of the social lives of things emphasizes the constructive, constitutive work involved in attaching and detaching symbolic meanings as material artefacts acquire and lose commodity status. In both these cases and in many more besides, social scientific attention routinely revolves around the position, status, ambition and capability of those who do the integrating. In keeping with Latour's (1987) methodological injunction, the tendency is to follow the actors. By contrast, our strategy is to follow the elements of practice and to track changing configurations over time.

This 'elemental' approach is unusual in provisionally de-centring the human actor (as integrator) but it is, at the same time, consistent with the argument that in the moment of doing, practitioners (those who do) simultaneously reproduce the practices in which they are engaged and the elements of which these practices are made. In Reckwitz's terms, the elements of a practice – those of which the 'block' is made – are linked in and through integrative moments of practice-as-performance (Reckwitz, 2002). By paying attention to the trajectories of elements, and to the making and breaking of links between them, it is, we suggest, possible to describe and analyse change and stability without prioritizing either agency or structure. In this chapter we explore the possibility and value of such an approach with reference to the history of car-driving. As might be expected, this generates as many questions as it resolves: for instance, do elements exist in several practices at once? Do the elements of which a practice is composed circulate and travel in ways that practices-as-entities do not? How do moments of localized integration relate to spatially distributed processes of diffusion and disappearance? Since these are themes developed in the rest of the book, this chapter has the dual function of setting the scene for further discussion and of introducing the first planks of what will become a more elaborate conceptual framework. Before taking another step in any such direction, we need to say more about what the elements of practice might be and about how we define them.

MATERIAL, COMPETENCE AND MEANING

In Chapter 1 we referred to Reckwitz's claim that practices consist of interdependencies between 'forms of bodily activities, forms of mental activities, "things" and their use, a background knowledge in the form of understanding, know-how, states of emotion and motivational knowledge' (2002: 249). With this catalogue as our starting point, we now put forward an even simpler scheme based on just three elements. The key features of this scheme are described below.

'Things' feature barely at all in the writings of Giddens (1984) or Bourdieu (1984), whose theories are indeed almost entirely 'social'. However, these aspects are important not only for Reckwitz but also for Schatzki who explores the various ways in which 'practices are intrinsically connected to and interwoven with objects' (2002: 106). In reviewing recent contributions to practice theory, Røpke (2009) suggests that there is now broad agreement that things should be treated as elements of practice. This is a position we share. 'Materials', encompassing objects, infrastructures, tools, hardware and the body itself, consequently figure as the first of the three elements on which we focus (Shove et al., 2007).

In most accounts, know-how, background knowledge and understanding are taken to be crucial whether in the form of what Giddens (1984) describes as practical consciousness, deliberately cultivated skill, or more abstractly, as shared understandings of good or appropriate performance in terms of which specific enactments are judged. Knowing in the sense of being able to evaluate a performance is not the same as knowing in the sense of having the skills required to perform, and in some situations this is an important distinction (Warde, 2005). For the purposes of this chapter, which is in essence about how links are made between the elements of which practices are composed, we lump multiple forms of understanding and practical knowledgeability together and simply refer to them as 'competence', our second element.

Our next simplifying move is to collapse what Reckwitz describes as mental activities, emotion and motivational knowledge into the one broad element of 'meaning', a term we use to represent the social and symbolic significance of participation at any one moment. This is tricky territory in that those who write about social practices are in much less agreement about how to characterize meaning, emotion and motivation. In Schatzki's analysis, 'teleoaffective' structures – embracing ends, projects, tasks, purposes, beliefs, emotions and moods (1996: 89) – are central to the organizing and ordering of practice and to the location of social practice within what Schatzki describes as 'timespace' (Schatzki, 2010b). He uses this concept to elaborate on the point that what people do has a history and a setting; to show that doings are future oriented, and that both aspects are united in the moment of performance. Instead of emphasizing the ongoing, unfolding character of ends and projects, we short-circuit this discussion and instead treat meaning as an element of practice, not something that stands outside or that figures as a motivating or driving force.

In what follows we work with the idea that practices are defined by interdependent relations between materials, competences and meanings. This deliberately streamlined approach has many advantages, but like all other such accounts it supposes that elements, however they might be defined, are somehow 'out there' in the world, waiting to be linked together. If we go along with the idea that practices exist when elements are integrated, we need to recognize two related possibilities: one is that relevant elements exist but without being linked (proto-practice); the second is that practices disintegrate when links are no longer sustained. Figure 2.1 illustrates these three scenarios.

This basic scheme reveals little about the nature of the linking entailed in keeping a practice together, it tells us nothing about who is involved, how access to relevant elements is distributed or how instances of integration themselves transform and generate new competences, meanings and materialities. However, it does underline the centrality of linkage: if specific configurations are to remain effective, connections between defining elements have to be renewed time and again. This suggests that stability and routinization are not end points of a linear process of normalization. Rather, they should be understood as ongoing accomplishments in which similar elements are repeatedly linked together in similar ways.

Having introduced the idea that practices consist of active integrations of material, competence and meaning, the rest of this chapter is designed to address two related questions. First, what do we gain by analysing the invention and disappearance of practices (as relatively enduring entities) with reference to the changing relationships between

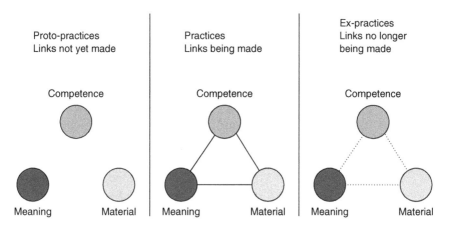

Figure 2.1   Proto-practices, practices and ex-practices

the elements of which they are, or were composed? Second, does this strategy allow us to analyse change in a manner that bridges between accounts of practices-as-performances and practices-as-entities? As promised, we address these questions with reference to the development of car-driving in part because this is a familiar, well documented practice that has developed fast and diffused widely during the last century. In addition, driving is remarkably standardized despite having taken hold through different routes and at different times in diverse countries and cultures. As will become clear, our approach is useful in conceptualizing commonality (a result of the circulation of elements) and local variation (in how these elements are integrated).

To reiterate, our opening propositions are that practices like driving a car depend on specific combinations of materials, meanings and competence; that driving evolves as these ingredients change; and that such changes are in part a consequence of the integrative work involved. In the paragraphs that follow we comment on different aspects of this process, showing how elements have been linked and how ties have been made and broken along the way. We do so not with the aim of providing a detailed or coherent history of driving but in order to show what an element-based approach has to offer.

CAR-DRIVING – ELEMENTS AND LINKAGES

Histories of the car and of its impact on society generally emphasize the extent to which petrol-driven vehicles have revolutionized the mobility of things and people, whether for good or ill (Miller, 2001). John Urry describes automobility as 'a self-organizing autopoietic, nonlinear system that spreads world-wide, and includes cars, car-drivers, roads, petroleum supplies and many novel objects, technologies and signs' (2004: 27). In generating 'the preconditions for its own self-expansion' (27), Urry claims that this system has totally reconfigured civil society, producing 'distinct ways of dwelling, travelling and socializing in and through an automobilised time-space' (Sheller and Urry, 2000: 737). By any standards this is a tale of rapid and radical change. But if we concentrate on the doing of driving, narrowly defined as controlling and navigating a car, the novelty is much less pronounced.

Many elements of driving pre-date the arrival of the car itself and in the early days, continuities with horse riding, cycling, machine operation and sea-faring (as in the red and green of traffic lights) were more evident than they are today. For example, the convention of travelling on the left-hand side of the road apparently has its origins in the need for ready use of a sword (typically wielded in the right hand). The switch to the right, which took place in some countries but not all, reportedly relates to the configuration of teams of wagon horses in the late 1700s. With the driver seated on the left rear horse (in order to lash the rest with a whip held in the right hand), it was easier to see the wheels of wagons going the other way if they passed on the left, hence driving on the right-hand side of the road (World Standards, 2011). Whatever their origin, rules of the road and related forms of *competence* crossed over from the world of the horse to that of the car, as did many *material* aspects of design. The first car bodies were, for instance, constructed by carriage builders accustomed to painstaking and customized forms of craft production. The structures they were used to making did not suit the new demands of a short wheelbase, and their working methods failed to deliver the forms of standardization required. Many adaptations were needed but many traditional features carried across and informed both the style and the format of powered vehicles (Gartman,

1994: 26). As these few examples suggest, materials and forms of competence migrated between co-existing practices to such an extent that the only really new element of car-driving in the USA in the early 1900s was the gasoline engine itself, along with knowledge of how to maintain and repair it.

By all accounts this knowledge was hard won and hard to come by. Although the first gasoline-powered internal combustion engines were somewhat easier to operate than their steam-driven cousins (Volti, 1996), they were extremely troublesome and prone to breaking down. Indeed, they were so awkward to operate that driving and repairing were in effect one and the same. Kevin Borg elaborates on this relation in his brilliant history of automechanics. He quotes the experience of a driver from 1900: 'As one enthusiast put it, to become a "complete master of the art of driving a self propelled vehicle . . . you must, in the first place, be a good mechanic"' (Borg, 1999: 804). Other telling indications of what doing driving then involved include the recommendation to carry 'bailing wire and a ball of twine as standard motoring accessories' (Borg, 2007: 15), along with an armoury of wrenches, pliers and chisels.

The specific configurations of materiality and competence that defined driving in the USA between 1895 and around 1906 limited the rate at which the practice spread and influenced the image of risk and adventure associated with it. In other words, the *relation* between requisite elements, and the relative scarcity of necessary competence, structured both the character of driving and the manner in which it took hold.

Not all wealthy car-owners were mechanically minded enough to 'drive', and a significant number employed their own chauffeurs to 'perform the duties of driver and of a mechanic: a "coachman" for their automobile', who would take 'responsibility for the vehicle's full-time care and maintenance' (Borg, 2007: 16–17). In social terms, the potential for turning coachmen into chauffeurs seemed promising enough: both provided services that enabled wealthy employers to travel. However, the dearth of technical proficiency confounded this simple transfer. Borg provides a fascinating account of the disruption that ensued. In his words, 'the knowledge and skills of animal husbandry did not necessarily translate into mechanical ability' (Borg, 2007: 18).

As new elements of know-how entered the frame, others like those involved in caring for horses were rendered redundant. For a time, necessary skills in metal and maintenance were in relatively short supply, and mechanics capable of keeping cars in repair and on the road were not necessarily content with the deferential service role accorded to them. Borg analyses shifting relationships between motor, mechanic and driver, and the emergence, typically from blacksmiths' shops, of organizational forms like the garage and the petrol station as signs and to some extent causes of a changing social hierarchy. In the context of the present discussion, this particularly awkward moment in the history of driving underlines the close-coupled relation between materiality and competence and the possibility that access to these equally essential elements is unequally and unevenly distributed.

Such interdependencies are, in turn, relevant for the social and symbolic significance of driving. To some extent, the meaning of the practice initially related to the prior identities of those who participated and to where and when driving was done. As a pursuit confined to those with wealth it signified affluence, but as more and different people took to the wheel so this image changed. However, there is more at stake than status. In the first years, the mechanical challenges were such that driving was, by definition, an adventure. As well as being thrilling and uncertain, driving slotted into what Gartman describes as 'the emerging therapeutic ethos of the American bourgeoisie' – an ethos in which the restorative valuing of fresh air, forced in at speed, gave car travel a distinctive appeal (1994: 34–35; Wolf, 1996: 194). This connection was not to last, but driving was, for a time, classified as one of a number of especially healthy pursuits. More abstractly, interpretations of the benefits and perils of driving are inherently unstable, being defined and evaluated with reference to an also changing set of alternatives like horse riding or cycling, along with related discourses of health, danger and environmental risk.

The preceding paragraphs draw attention to threads of continuity, emphasizing the extent to which elements of driving carried over or were carried between different practices (cycling, horse riding, driving). They describe processes of lopsided development – for a while, the scarcity of mechanical expertise structured and stifled the doing of driving – and they demonstrate that relations between the elements of

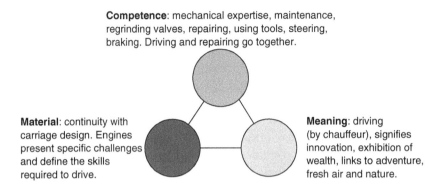

Competence: mechanical expertise, maintenance, regrinding valves, repairing, using tools, steering, braking. Driving and repairing go together.

Material: continuity with carriage design. Engines present specific challenges and define the skills required to drive.

Meaning: driving (by chauffeur), signifies innovation, exhibition of wealth, links to adventure, fresh air and nature.

Figure 2.2   Elements of driving in the USA in the 1900s–1910s

which driving is made are constantly on the move: new links are made as others are broken.

In theory, one might represent the development of driving (or any other practice) through a series of snapshots, each capturing the materials, meanings and competences involved at different moments. Figure 2.2 provides a simple sketch of the elements of which driving was made in the USA in the first decade of the twentieth century.

Other similar images representing driving from the 1910s through to the present day would give a sense of the 'elemental' histories involved and of the succession of composite entities of which the history of driving is formed. Since we are interested in methods of analysing and conceptualizing the dynamics of social practice, and not the history of driving as such, we use the next few sections to explore the limits and benefits of characterizing stability and change in these terms.

MAKING LINKS

If practices are composed of materials, meanings and competences, histories of practice need to take note of the conjunction of *all three elements at once*. In this they differ from conventional histories of the development and diffusion of cars, many of which focus on technical and organizational innovations in manufacturing and on Ford's contribution in particular

(Wolf, 1996; Gartman, 2004). Mass production and increasing affordability were surely important but our element-based approach suggests that the availability of a car was not, in itself, sufficient, and that the relation between competence and materiality was just as critical. As illustrated in Figure 2.2, there was a point when driving was of necessity concentrated in the hands of a few for reasons that had to do with knowledge as well as wealth. Industry commentators of the time were in a sense right in thinking that the car had a limited future for exactly this reason: 'In 1900, the German car company Daimler-Benz was predicting total European demand for cars at fewer than 1,500, the number of families the company estimated would be able to afford a chauffeur' (Kreitzman, 1999: 52).

As it happens, the way forward was not via a sudden influx of chauffeurs. Instead, material relations were reconfigured such that driving required different, less demanding skills. It is certainly true that cars of different vintage 'script' and structure the manner in which they are used: they make some kinds of driving possible and prevent others. It is also true that within science and technology studies much has been written about material–human relations and 'user-practices' (Oudshoorn and Pinch, 2005). Although concepts of domestication and appropriation are useful in understanding when and why technologies are rejected or taken up, further steps are required to show what these processes mean for the trajectory of driving an emergent entity.

As cars became more reliable and easier to operate, certain capacities passed from person to machine. There are many such examples, but automatic starting and signalling are some of the most obvious. Borg summarizes the implications:

> In order to appeal to a broader market, many American automakers began to focus on producing moderate- and low-priced cars that would meet the needs of businessmen, tradesmen, and farmers. These new motorists could not afford, and did not desire, the services of a chauffeur mechanic. They pushed the American automobile industry to produce more reliable cars for owners in all social classes. As reliability increased, the technical demands that initially favored the use of chauffeurs decreased.

> (Borg, 1999: 821)

In Latour's terms, know-how previously embodied in the mechanic-driver was delegated to the vehicle itself. To understand what this means for driving, it is, we suggest, necessary to show how this dynamic relation reconstitutes the *meaning* of the practice. As long as driving was defined as a leisure pursuit favoured by the mechanically minded rich, the challenge of completing a journey without breaking down was arguably part of the fun. However, when car owners became drivers and when they viewed driving as a means of making outings and sharing these experiences with friends and family, 'mechanical demands became a distraction, a nuisance, possibly even an embarrassment' (Borg, 1999: 805). As indicated here, elements of meaning and materiality also co-evolve.

If we take the practice of driving rather than the car or the driver as the central unit of enquiry, it becomes clear that relations between the vehicle (along with the road and other traffic), the know-how required to keep it in motion and the meaning and significance of driving and passengering are intimately related, so much so that they constitute what Reckwitz refers to as a 'block' of interconnected elements. Accordingly, novelty can come from any quarter and at any time.

Merriman (2006) describes one such disruptive moment. In the 1960s in the UK, the introduction of multi-lane roads (motorways) threw elements of what was by then an already established practice out of synch, reopening debate about the relation between car and driver. Critically, multi-lane driving meant looking behind and not just ahead:

> Would Britain's drivers, many of whom had little or no experience of driving on multi-lane dual carriageway roads, know which lane to drive in, stay in one lane, or check their mirrors when overtaking? Would they or their vehicles be able to cope with the high speeds that were possible and legal with the absence of a speed limit? Would they understand the new signs or be able to negotiate flyover junctions safely?
>
> (Merriman, 2006: 77)

Driving soon re-stabilized, doing so in ways that incorporated new techniques including those of checking the mirror. This is not the end of the

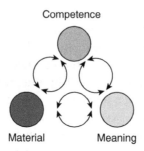

Figure 2.3   Elements shape each other

story: much else has happened since the 1960s. Developments in soft-ware and in ergonomics have reworked how 'automobility is practiced' and produced new variants of 'embodied practices of driving and "pas-sengering"' (Thrift, 2004: 46) such innovations being, as Preda puts it, part of a 'continuous process of reciprocal adaptation of practical skills and materialized knowledge' (1999: 351).

We have already said that new practices involve novel combinations of new or existing elements. To this we now add that such integrations are themselves transformative: material, meaning and competence are not just interdependent, they are also mutually shaping, as is indicated in Figure 2.3.

In introducing Figure 2.2, we suggested that histories of practice might be represented in the form of a chronological sequence of cross-sections, each revealing the character of the elements involved at differ-ent moments. Figure 2.4 takes this idea a stage further, suggesting that practice-historians might also follow individual elements as they change over time.

In this section we have commented on how the elements of driving are inter-linked and on how these connections change. Although convincing enough in its own terms, this account generates a number of puzzling and potentially troublesome problems.

First, the pathways traced in Figure 2.4 suggest that innovations in practice leave trails of abandoned and disconnected elements behind – is this really so, and if it is, when and how do elements disappear?

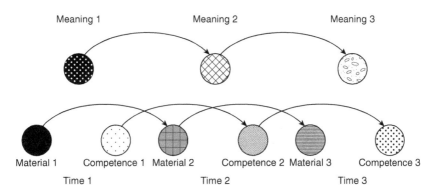

Figure 2.4   Elements of practice change over time

How are we to conceptualize the processes involved? Second, Figure 2.3 shows how the elements of a single practice interconnect and shape each other, but what does this mean for other practices in which the same or similar elements are also a part? Associations between driving and masculinity suggest that elements can, on occasion, bridge between different practices with the result that changes born of one integration have consequences for others. Third, Figures 2.3 and 2.4 are abstract sketches and as such provide no sense of scale. There is consequently more to say about how elements travel and about the necessarily localized sites and moments of their integration. Finally, if we are to think about change over time we need to think about how the characteristics of driving, defined by previous generations, structure the careers and experiences of contemporary carriers and practitioners.

In discussing each of these topics in turn, the next few sections introduce themes addressed in greater detail in each of the chapters that follow.

BREAKING LINKS

If we view practices as ongoing integrations of elements, we need to consider what happens when requisite connections are no longer made.

More specifically, when and how are links broken and what is the fate of elements that are stranded as a result?

Histories of motoring frequently refer to materials that used to be part of driving but which are not part of the practice as it is currently configured. By the mid-1920s drivers no longer needed to 'bundle up', put on special clothing (coats, goggles and gloves) or pack bailing wire and twine before setting off (Sachs and Reneau, 1992: 133). These previously essential bits of hardware had different fates: some became part of other practices (driving gloves became just gloves); others (goggles) were discarded, ending up in museums, on eBay or reclassified as rubbish (Strasser, 1999). From this perspective, understanding the changing materiality of doing, not only of driving but of other practices too, is important for understanding the flow of goods within and between societies. We discuss the wider implications of this observation in Chapter 3. For now it is enough to notice first, that we live alongside the material traces of practices past (coaching inns, canal networks, tollgate cottages), and second that rates of obsolescence and re-appropriation are part and parcel of the dynamics of practice.

But what of competences and meanings, what happens to these when no longer integrated in practice? As we all know, competences can lie dormant, persisting in the memory for years without being activated, or being at least partly preserved in written form – in recipes, manuals and instructions. On special occasions techniques like those involved in starting a Ford Model T on a cold day are brought back to life – videos of this procedure are now available on the Internet. However, instances in which antiquated skills are resurrected are probably better seen as elements of 'doing history' than of 'doing driving' as it is known today. There is, then, a sense in which driving is usefully conceptualized as an ongoing, irreversible process of collective forgetting: forgetting how to manage oil and grease; forgetting the full language of hand-signals (in the UK, hand-signals were dropped from the driving test in 1975: Mail online, 2005); and, with satellite navigation, forgetting how to read a map.

The direction this takes is not without consequence in that patterns of knowing and not-knowing, and the distribution of expertise, ignorance and amnesia, are related both to each other and to the ordinary politics of practice. Cars, once important sites of amateur expertise, have been re-designed to prevent tinkering and ensure that relevant knowledge is concentrated in the hands of a very few (e.g. garages with relevant computer diagnostics etc.). People may retain skills acquired through what Borg (2007) refers to as 'under hood' activity, but be prevented from putting these into practice by the sealed boxes of electronic tricks of which cars are constituted today. From this we draw the more general conclusion that the changing salience of specific techniques, and the redundancy of others, is an outcome of what people do (i.e. of personal trajectories and careers) and in collective terms, a precondition for what they might do next, individually and at a societal level.

Elements of meaning also come and go. In reviewing the car's cultural history, Gartman describes three generic moments: one associated with social class and distinction; one in which individuality and customization are key; and one in which cars are positioned in terms of a multiplicity of lifestyle sub-cultures (Gartman, 2004). Other writers describe the changing status of driving as a utilitarian or luxurious experience and discuss its association, in some times and places, with youth, rebellion and Westernization (Garvey, 2001; O'Dell, 2001; Siegelbaum, 2008). As represented in this literature, forms of social significance seem to accumulate: one layer being added to the next, with the result that previous meanings are overlain rather than obliterated or dissolved.

These observations suggest that when links are broken, and when forms of driving evolve, materials, meanings and forms of competence disappear in characteristically different ways: vanishing with little or no trace, remaining dormant or taking on a new lease of life within and as part of other practices.

ELEMENTS BETWEEN PRACTICES

This far we have considered the making and breaking of links between the various elements of which driving is composed. In taking this approach we have paid no attention to related practices, or to the possibility that the elements involved have an existence beyond the doing of driving. This is an important omission. As we have just seen, driving has at times been associated with concepts like those of Westernization, youth or masculinity, all of which are defined and constituted through their 'participation' in many practices at once.

Do shared elements bridge between different practices, and if so with what consequences for the different pursuits of which they are a part? In relation to driving, Volti claims that the novelty, speed and unreliability of the first cars were important in framing driving as a dashing and exciting thing to do. As such driving acquired characteristics already 'intertwined with masculine culture' (Volti, 1996: 667). Kline and Pinch make a similar argument, suggesting that

> competence in the operation and repair of the machinery formed a defining element of masculinity ... Consequently, the gasoline automobile, which was symbolically inscribed for masculine use ... came onto farmsteads headed, in general, by men partly because of their technical competence.
>
> (Kline and Pinch, 1996: 779)

In both accounts, notions of masculinity provide a point of connection between practices of repairing and driving. This is not a stable relationship. As driving becomes less thrilling and less mechanically demanding, its significance for gendered identity shifts. In the same moment, the meaning of masculinity evolves. Figure 2.5 illustrates this double movement.

As this figure suggests, links are made and broken not only between the elements that constitute a single practice (driving), but also between the multiple practices of which similar elements are a part (driving and repairing). In the case considered here, associations with masculinity (part of the element of meaning represented at the centre of the Figure) are formed by and constitutive of at least two practices at once: driving on the one hand, and repairing on the other.

This hints at a much more elaborate picture in which diverse elements circulate within and between many different practices, constituting a form of connective tissue that holds complex social arrangements in place, and potentially pulls them apart. To the extent that this is so, the attaching and detaching of meaning and signification sends ripples

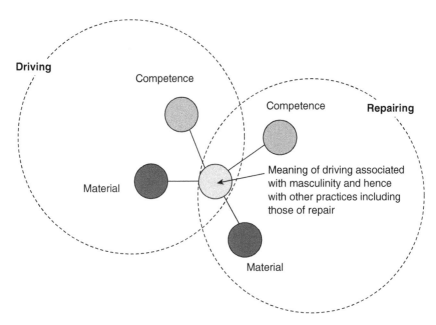

Figure 2.5   Elements between practices

across the cultural landscape as a whole. Something similar happens when forms of competence circulate (as when skills transfer) and when material elements figure in more than one practice at a time.

STANDARDIZATION AND DIVERSITY

In describing the evolution of driving we have assumed that at any one moment it is a relatively homogeneous affair. Although analytically convenient, and perhaps necessary if we are to describe change over time, it is important to recognize that multiple ways of 'doing' driving co-exist. In so far as the practice has *a* history, this is of necessity a composite narrative in which diverse experiences, some rural, some urban; some rooted in American culture, others defined by the very different infrastructures of Europe, or Asia, are, for the sake of argument, folded together. If we were to take these different trajectories into account, we might notice that driving took hold earlier and faster in France, a country which had a good road structure and petrol distribution system, than it did in the UK, and that in both these countries and in Germany cars tended to be more compact than in the USA. Furthermore, driving in modern urban India or in rural Finland represents a blend of elements that differs significantly, in history and in detail, from those of which the practice is made in the Pitjantjatjara lands of Southern Australia. Here, driving encompasses prior traditions of navigation including reference to the sun and to tracking, initially of animals and now of tyre marks. According to Young, travelling by car fits into and in a sense reinforces specific spiritual connections with the land (2001).

So does it make sense to talk of 'driving' as a recognizable entity? The answer is yes and no. It is 'yes' in that certain elements of the practice – especially the car itself – are remarkably standardized. Car production is strongly influenced by a 'dominant' design, the shared features of which mean that people who have learned to drive are capable of operating a huge range of vehicles around the world. There is, in addition, an established, internationally agreed set of conventions regarding driving licences, road signage and symbols. These do not guarantee consistency, nor do they necessarily overrule local convention. In India slower moving traffic sticks to the side of the road, giving priority to the largest vehicles, that are in turn expected to give way to animals (Edensor, 2004). Even so, cars, rules and other aspects of infrastructure – conventions of road engineering, the design of bridges, service and petrol stations and so on – hold repertoires of driving together in ways that reproduce a certain commonality of experience. According to Urry, the global road network has consequently become a special setting in which strangers 'follow such shared rules, communicate through common sets of visual and aural signals, and interact even without eye-contact in a kind of default space or nonplace available to all "citizens of the road"' (2006: 21).

One way of making sense of the relation between standardization and persistent diversity is to suggest that practices like driving are 'homegrown' in the sense that each instance of doing is informed by previous, related and associated practices. At the same time, each instance is to a large extent defined by the elements of which it is composed. Manufacturers, governments, driving schools and international associations are consequently instrumental in circulating common forms of competence, meaning and materiality. In so doing they contribute to the standardization of driving as it is reproduced in different locations.

This distinction between elements – which can and do travel – and practices, viewed as necessarily localized, necessarily situated instances of integration (which do not travel) is useful in making sense of the roles consumers, producers and governments play in the reproduction and diffusion of different ways of life (Shove and Pantzar, 2005: 62). We return to this topic in Chapter 8, 'Promoting transitions in practice', but for the time being, it is enough to notice that institutions involved in developing or circulating the elements of which practices are made rarely control the manner in which they are combined.

INDIVIDUAL AND COLLECTIVE CAREERS

As we have shown, the elements of driving continue to evolve. This is important in defining the practices into which novices are drawn. Those who became drivers in the UK in the 1960s entered and contributed to the development of a practice the characteristics and qualities of which are unlike those that pertain today. People who pass their test in 2012 consequently encounter – and will in turn help to shape – what is in many, but not all, respects a substantially different entity. The fact that driving is constituted by, and takes place in the midst of the routines and habits of other road users, all of whom have 'careers' of different duration, reminds us that the lives of practitioners and practices intersect. In short, there is something emergent and collective about driving (and other practices) which has to do with the relation between many co-existing performances situated alongside and in the context of collectively accumulated experience. Elias touches on this in his description of driving as a type of collective self-regulation, the details of which are shaped by many diverse and distributed instances of 'diffuse experimentation by a number of people' (1995: 16). In his words:

Controlling the car (including maintaining it) is nothing but an extension of the driver's self-control or self-regulation. The pattern of self-regulation by a driver at the wheel of his car, however, is determined to a large extent by the social standard that society in every country has developed for the individual self-regulation of the men and women who drive cars.

(Elias, 1995: 25)

We do not need to go along with Elias' broader argument about the relation between technology and civilization to accept that individual drivers contribute to a trajectory of development that is simultaneously defined by others and at the same time reconfigured, in some tiny way, by each journey they make. Chapter 4, 'Recruitment, defection and reproduction', takes this discussion further and provides a more detailed account of how people become the carriers of practice and of how practices change through related processes of recruitment, defection and reproduction.

In this chapter we have used the case of car driving to develop and explore our two opening propositions – that social practices consist of elements that are integrated when practices are enacted, and that practices emerge, persist and disappear as connections between defining elements are made and broken. Our first move was to identify and then work with three broad categories of elements, namely materials, meanings and competences. This deliberately simple representation of practices allowed us to concentrate on our main task, which was to describe and discuss the making and breaking of links.

Rather than writing about the lives and ambitions of those who do the integrating, we have taken these elements and their interconnection as our central topic. The suggestion that practices consist of elements that are bound together through doing makes sense, but as we have seen, this implies that materials, meanings and competences have lives that extend before and after these moments of integration. The related idea that we are surrounded by the fragments and disconnected remains of practices past is odd, and a bit disturbing, but it is also consistent with the position we have developed this far. It is, in addition, in keeping with our representation of early forms of 'driving' as an amalgam of elements, many of which were already well established, for instance through horse riding and cycling.

In describing further developments in the doing of driving we drew attention to the ways in which elements configure each other. In the early days, drivers needed a wealth of mechanical knowledge to keep their vehicles in motion. During the first decades of motoring, this interface between materiality and competence was radically 're-scripted'. Cars became more reliable and in the same move, less was required of the driver. Developments like these proved vital: if driving was to become established as a normal practice, the necessary competences had to be mastered by many, and not just a few. Equally, as more and different people took to the wheel, so the meaning of driving evolved. Precisely because of these interdependencies, the elements of driving never stand still. These observations led us to conclude that driving and the elements of which it is made constitute each other. Put simply, configurations that work (i.e. practices) do so because material elements and those of meaning and competence are linked together, and transformed, *through* the process of doing.

These provisional conclusions bring new questions into view. Do elements have what one might think of as a life of their own? Do they die, or are they only ever transformed? Exactly how do they circulate and travel? These are topics to which we now turn, reserving others, including questions about how people become the carriers of practice and how practices link together, for later.

3

THE LIFE OF ELEMENTS

In Chapter 2 we argued that practices like driving develop as links between defining elements are made and broken. In so far as this is true, the potential for practices to spread and take hold depends, at least in part, on the ready availability of requisite elements. If we are to understand how practices are distributed within and between societies, we need to think about how materials, meanings and forms of competence circulate and persist. This requires a shift of emphasis. Whereas Chapter 2 concentrated on connections between elements, this chapter discusses what one might think of as generic features or 'elemental' characteristics. In proceeding as if these could be somehow separated out, and in suggesting that materials, meanings and competences travel and endure in distinctly different ways, we seem to go against the grain of the previous chapter, in which we made much of the point that elements constitute each other and change *through processes of integration.* This is no accident. By moving between analytic frames, some chapters prioritizing links and connections, others concentrating on elements, practitioners or forms of feedback, we examine the dynamics of practice from different angles. At the same time, we try to keep sight of the interdependencies involved.

This is a tricky course to steer, but as mentioned in Chapter 2, elements do seem to travel in ways that practices do not. As structured and situated arrangements, practices are always in the process of formation, re-formation and de-formation. By contrast, elements are comparatively stable and are, as such, capable of circulating between places and enduring over time. We are consequently surrounded by things that have outlived the practices of which they were once a vital part (Shove and Pantzar, 2006). Abandoned biscuit presses, outdated computer equipment and tools for tasks no longer undertaken are obvious examples, but understandings, meanings and types of expertise are also discarded as practices evolve. Changing systems of provision have clearly undermined the importance of knowing how to darn socks, maintain a car or bake fancy biscuits at home. But as some of these examples demonstrate, seemingly defunct skills are occasionally res-urrected: in some circles baking is a newly popular thing to do. At the same time, the meaning of home baking as a daily duty has probably changed for good. As hinted at here and discussed in greater detail at the end of this chapter, elements seem to 'last' in different ways.

In thinking about how elements move we reach a similar conclusion. In describing some of the forms of transportation, codification and classifica-tion involved, this chapter contributes to the overall project of understand-ing when, where and how practices emerge, diffuse, persist and disappear. However contrived it might be, the method of treating elements as if they had a life of their own is useful in understanding the history and social geography of what people do. Since we need to keep parallel accounts in play we must remember that it is only through their integration in practice that elements are reproduced, eroded or carried from one setting or popu-lation to another. With these cautions in place we can now move on.

MODES OF CIRCULATION

In theory it would be possible to plot the reach and range of specific practices on a map. Such an exercise could be used to identify places (cities, regions, countries) where baseball is a majority interest (Wang, 2007), where it is normal to shower at least once a day, or where people have toast for breakfast. Should such maps exist they would reveal locations in which necessary elements co-exist. For example, toast eat-ing depends upon bread of a certain type and size; a toaster; a concept of breakfast in which toast is included; and a measure of toast-related competence (Molotch, 2003). Rather than imagining one map of prac-tice, we might therefore think of three separate layers – one depicting the distribution of requisite competence, another showing access to necessary materials, and a third plotting the prevalence of toast as a meaningful part of breakfast. Having toast in the morning is only pos-sible where all three layers overlap. In all other situations one or more of the necessary ingredients is missing; for example, toasters are not available, the bread is absent or not of a form that would go in the toaster, or toasters and bread both exist but not the convention of mak-ing breakfast at home. The fact that requisite elements co-exist does not guarantee that they will be linked together, but the potential is there.

In considering the diffusion of practice – how did toast eating become established and how did the practice spread? – it is evidently important to analyse the distribution of constitutive elements and to understand how they travel. The next three sections describe some of the modes of circulation involved, starting with transportation.

Transportation and access: material

For many years, methods and styles of building reflected the local avail-ability of natural resources like timber, stone or clay. According to Manzini and Cau (1989), vernacular traditions of design and construc-tion have been eroded by the importation of 'foreign' materials and correspondingly foreign ways of using them. In this analysis the capacity to ship goods around the world has reconfigured the doing of building, and has done so on a global scale. As this rather obvious example sug-gests, the movement of material elements of practice often involves their physical relocation. As such, trucks, trains, boats and planes have an important part to play in facilitating the circulation of goods and in establishing the contours of potential practice.

Some things are very much heavier or more awkward to move than others; again an obvious point, but again one that is relevant in thinking about how maps of material availability and sociotechnical potential are configured. Although not written with this in mind, Harris's history of the production and diffusion of cast-iron stoves provides a fine illustration of the close-coupled relation between infrastructures of mobility and comfort. In the USA in 1820, cast-iron stoves were viewed as 'an expensive item of restricted utility, and thus in limited demand'. Just 30 years later, they had become 'the first consumer durable with near-universal market penetration – available, affordable, versatile, and reliable' (Harris, 2008: 337). Harris's explanation is as follows:

> From the 1820s through at least the 1840s, unless consumers lived a relatively short wagon trip away from a navigable waterway, the ability of most of them to buy heavy, bulky goods, or those with a low value-to-weight ratio, from any but local makers and suppliers, was quite restricted. Similar considerations applied to the manufacture of such goods: from the 1810s through the 1830s, for example, the making of heavy cast-iron products like stoves stayed tied to the blast furnaces providing their raw material, i.e. it was more or less confined to those locations where iron ore from mines or bogs, flux (limestone or sea-shells), and fuel (generally charcoal) could be sourced close to one another.
>
> (Harris, 2008: 340)

As described here, canal systems and railway routes opened the way for more complex and more specialized systems of provision, innovation and distribution, releasing stove makers and potential stove buyers from the basic constraints of heavy material geography. Harris argues that this was crucial for the development and diffusion of stoves that were in turn essential in redefining the meaning and practice of comfort:

> Without a sustained, multilayered improvement in the means for transporting information and goods around the country, the rapid development of a nationwide stove market between the 1830s and 1850s could not have taken place, and no general transformation of the American indoor climate would have happened.
>
> (Harris, 2008: 349)

Not all material elements of practice are quite as weighty as a cast-iron stove and since it is in any case *access* that matters, sites of production are often as important as modes of transportation. In 1854, 30,329 packages of corrugated iron were exported from England to the Australian state of Victoria as emigrants arrived with their future dwellings packed, in kit form, in the holds of ships. This mass movement of metal came to a halt when a sheet rolling and galvanizing works was established in Newcastle, Australia in 1921. By 1939 this and one other plant produced almost all Australia's galvanized sheeting (Warr, 2000). The fact that corrugated iron rusts, and that sheets need replacing, reminds us of the further point that many practices depend on supplies of consumables as well as on more durable objects, tools and infrastructures. Staying with this example, practices that involve corrugated iron (like constructing a shed) are also likely to require an array of related materials including timber, nails, screws and fixings, each of which have different histories and geographies of production and distribution. To complicate matters, while it is sometimes possible to use alternatives or substitutes, swapping nails for screws, many material components have what Akrich (1992) describes as a 'closed' script, meaning that their role, and relation to other artefacts, is tightly defined. By these means material arrangements configure each other, frequently doing so in ways that are of relevance for who has access to what. In Chapter 2 we noticed that cars have been (re)designed to prevent amateur tinkering. On a different scale, the design and operation of infrastructures, mains water systems, cities and transportation networks reflect and structure inequalities of access and hence the social distribution of different practices. Graham and Marvin's (2001) argument that urban networks are becoming increasingly exclusive is relevant in this regard.

As these few comments indicate, the topic of how and where things move, and how access to them is structured, is vast. In touching on processes involved, our aim is not to track the freight of the world or identify the very many ways in which material elements of practice are distributed, accumulated, managed or policed. Rather, the point is to recognize that whereas forms of (co)location, transportation and access are typically important for the diffusion of material elements, forms of competence and meaning circulate in characteristically different ways.

Abstraction, reversal and migration: competence

In everyday life, learning through doing goes on all the time and often without noticing. While some skills can be picked up in this way, others require much more deliberate effort, sometimes involving hours of dedicated training. For any one individual, the experience and process of becoming a competent practitioner is important, but for the purposes of this chapter we take the element of know-how and competence as our unit of enquiry rather than the persons involved, whether as recipients, translators, mediators or sources. Since we are interested in the circulation and distribution of elements, we concentrate especially on cases in which know-how travels beyond the confines of face-to-face interaction between master and apprentice, teacher and pupil or parent and child. In other words, we step back from situated practice-specific instances of learning-by-doing in order to consider how competences circulate *between* practices as well as between people. We begin by suggesting that concepts of abstraction and reversal are useful, and unusual, in describing processes that apply equally well to the analysis of practices as moments of performance and to the conceptualization of practices as recognizable entities.

The basic idea that knowledge has to be 'abstracted' from a local situation before it can travel, and that it needs to be 'reversed' when it arrives in some new destination, complicates popular interpretations of knowledge transfer as a simple process of sending and receiving. This representation is, however, consistent with an account of practices as integrative performances in which elements are conjoined. The suggestion that abstracted knowledge circulates between such moments or sites of enactment is also relevant in thinking about how competences circulate.

Theories of abstraction and reversal depend on distinguishing between local understanding on the one hand, and what Disco and van der Meulen (1998) term 'global-level cognitive constructs' on the other. As these authors explain, such constructs constitute forms of 'cosmopolitan' knowledge, that is, knowledge that has been disembedded from its local origins and is consequently capable of travelling widely whilst maintaining its own integrity. As discussed in Chapter 2, this idea brings with it the related, and somewhat strange, image of knowledge temporarily existing in limbo, contained in what Arie Rip describes as a dislocated holding tank or reservoir. In his words, 'knowledge products are delivered into a knowledge reservoir, carried by what one might call an epistemic community, and knowledge users pick up their own new combinations from the reservoir' (1998). This vision of a gigantic depot of abstracted, de-contextualized but not yet re-embedded knowledge is intriguing, as is the related suggestion that resources like libraries and the Internet, along with material objects and systems of regulation and certification, harbour pools of knowledge that have been variously certified, legitimated and prepared for travel.

The qualities and characteristics of the reservoir are surely relevant, but given that our aim is to understand how competences move, we focus on what 'has to be done to make knowledge movable (decontextualization and packaging), to let it move (infrastructure) and to make it work elsewhere (recontextualization, standardization)' (Deuten, 2003: 18).

Never mind what the range of relevant and available resources includes, the potential for effective circulation is limited by the capacity to 'reverse' or de-code packages of cosmopolitan knowledge. As Duguid puts it, 'Codification is remarkably powerful, but its power is only realized through the corresponding knowing how' (2005: 114). Duguid goes on to suggest that the necessary knowing how (i.e. knowing how to decode) is unevenly distributed because it is itself an outcome of prior experience. This suggests know-how can only travel – by means of abstraction and reversal – to sites in which practitioners are already prepared to receive it because of prior, first-hand, practice-based experience.

If the preparation, reversal and effective appropriation of abstracted knowledge depends on highly localized practice-based expertise, processes of movement are perhaps not as generically cosmopolitan as Rip and as Disco and van der Meulen suggest. To put it another way, the distribution and extent of the capacity to decode is itself dynamic and practice-based. Deuten's (2003) analysis of the standardization and diffusion of reinforced concrete as a reliable building material shows how this works.

Before reinforced concrete could be adopted as normal, many people had to become familiar with its qualities and with the conditions and circumstances of its effective use. This was especially challenging in that the properties of concrete differ from one batch to the next because of the variable nature of the raw materials involved and the conditions in which they are mixed and applied. In the early days, concrete expertise was craft-based, embedded and locally reproduced. As knowledge of the material became more widely shared it also (and in the same move) stabilized to the point that it could be defined, taught and learned regardless of the situation. Subsequent developments in standard speci-fications and regulation have the further effect of stabilizing what counts as expertise and of shaping both the nature of reinforced concret-ing and the first-hand experience-based competences of those involved.

It is true that agreed recipes and precisely codified testing regimes (i.e. abstracted knowledge) had to be in place before the practice of rein-forced concrete construction could be established and routinized on any scale. It is also clear that the codification of relevant knowledge is important for how recruitment to a practice is organized (novice con-crete contractors can now be taught *en masse*); for what practitioners actually do; what they learn in the process; and how reinforced concret-ing is reproduced and potentially transformed. To this Deuten adds the further point that the capacity to read and work with such recipes itself requires cultivation. In his words, 'to understand translocality, the methods, practices, instrumentations and technologies through which translocal knowledge is manifested have to be taken into account' (2003: 58). From this point of view, processes of sharing and standardizing knowledge are not merely channels through which competences spread, but are themselves part of the narrative of technological development.

This subtle analysis emphasizes the co-existence of localized and cos-mopolitan knowledges and their mutual interdependence. It also sug-gests that elements of knowledge – in this case, how to make and use reinforced concrete – are transformed by and also transform the several practices of which they are a part. Standardized knowledge of concrete production was, for instance, critical in facilitating the rapid uptake of reinforced concrete construction with implications for architecture, design and style, as well as for the practicalities of working on site.

Deuten's project was to describe the work involved in 'cosmopolitaniz-ing' concrete technology and in making it available in many locations, not to show how related forms of knowing and doing rippled out across neighbouring professional domains. But for us this is an interesting question. Do such movements depend on similar sequences of abstraction and reversal? Are other processes involved?

The concept of transferable skills is relevant in this regard. Having been mastered in one setting, competences like those of controlling a ball or speaking in public can be carried over and reproduced in others. People who are familiar with social situations like formal meetings or birthday parties can deploy and adapt this knowledge when participating in variants of these generic forms. This does not necessarily involve recognizable stages of abstraction and codification. Instead, specific competences are transferable because they are *common*, or at least common enough to a number of different practices. The potential for know-how to accumulate, circulate and travel sideways in this manner consequently depends on the degree to which diverse practices correspond. How are such commonalities established and at what level do they occur?

During the nineteenth century, techniques of rational planning and work efficiency along with specific methods of management, record-keeping and financial control travelled from office to home. Popular texts like *The Homemaker and Her Job* (Gilbreth, 1927) and *Scientific Management in the Home: Household engineering* (Frederick, 1920) were quite explicit about the source of their inspiration and about the benefits and values of running the home according to principles borrowed from the world of work. Appropriating techniques like those of time-and-motion studies and producing variants of economics suited to the home required a measure of culturally and historically specific adaptation (Jerram, 2006). One might therefore argue that elements of competence were abstracted from the world of work, codified in the form of manuals and instruction, and subsequently reversed into the domains of home, or more recently personal health.

However, this is not the only possible explanation. At a very practical level, Parr (1999) and Cowan (1983) make the point that concepts of rational and efficient management were actively promoted by companies keen to position new appliances as necessary tools for the proper ordering of domestic life. For this to work, family life had to be framed as a certain kind of project. This suggests that commonality had to be actively built at the level of ideas and discourses *before* related forms of know-how could be transferred.

From a more Foucauldian perspective, corporate success in this endeavour depended upon and at the same time reproduced generic techniques of self-regulation. By implication, methods of record-keeping, monitoring and discipline were capable of travelling across different areas of daily life because they tapped into (and formed) an underlying self-regulatory substructure. Developing these ideas, certain elements of know-how bridge between practices not by means of abstraction and reversal but by somehow constituting – and potentially changing – the texture and the quality of the social fabric in which many such practices are rooted. In their analysis of changing modes of governmentality, Miller and Rose (2008) address similar issues. Having identified 'ways of categorizing persons, rearrangements of factory layouts, treatments for various disorders, the testing of various groups or populations and so on', they go on to suggest that these represent 'multiple centres of calculation and authority that traverse and link up personal, social and economic life' (2008: 20). We explore the potential for characterizing societies in terms of types of linkage of which they are constituted in Chapter 6, 'Circuits of reproduction', but for the moment it is enough to recognize that these ties are important in establishing conditions of transferability and possibilities of exchange between one practice and another.

So far we have argued that forms of competence travel in ways that materials do not. Know-how is not typically moved by lorry or ship. Instead, relevant processes include those of abstraction, reversal, lateral migration and cross-practice creep. Second, and again in contrast to material objects that have a single physical location even when dormant, elements of knowledge can be contained for a time in virtual and actual reservoirs, depots and memories, persisting in this form between and beyond moments of practical enactment. Third, elements of know-how are typically modified, reconfigured and adapted as they move from one situation or person to another and as they circulate between practices. Finally, it seems that competences can only be transferred effectively in certain circumstances. As we have noticed, the capacity to decode is unequally distributed and itself born of previous practice-based experience. This is relevant for the ways in which competences accumulate and build during the course of an individual's life (see Chapter 4, 'Recruitment, defection and reproduction'). It is also critical for the 'life' of individual elements: for how they travel, for their availability within and between different social groups, and hence for the settings in which they might be integrated in practice.

Association and classification: meaning

For Miller and Rose (2008), and for Foucault, discourse and technique are so closely entwined that it makes little sense to separate them. But if we are to persist with our analytic method of distinguishing between the elements of which practices are made, we need to press on and ask whether there is anything distinctive about how meanings and images circulate and move. This is a huge topic and in order to make any headway at all we need to make other radically simplifying moves. One is to concentrate on instances in which interpretations and symbolic associations are relatively uncontested. A second is to play down the fact that attributions of meaning are unavoidably relative, situated and emergent. These steps allow us to proceed with a discussion of how elements of meaning diffuse and of what this means for the circulation of practices in and of which they are a part.

Although we are primarily interested in following the lives of elements, not of practices as such, a brief account of how Nordic Walking (a form of walking involving the use of two specially designed poles to increase the intensity of the exercise) emerged in Finland provides some insight into the ways in which meanings like those of infirmity and wellbeing 'travel' and evolve. For Nordic Walking to take hold on any scale, walking with 'sticks' had to be disassociated from meanings of frailty and somehow connected to concepts of vitality and wellbeing. This required a process of de- and re-classification: old connotations had to be shaken off and new connections made. In an effort to make this happen, manufacturers and others with an interest in establishing the practice sought to position it with reference to two established narratives, one of personal health, the other of fresh air, nature and outdoor life (Shove and Pantzar, 2005).

Two aspects of this story are relevant for a discussion of meaning. First, this semiotic positioning of Nordic Walking was only possible because concepts of wellbeing and nature already existed in the popular imagination, each having recognizable qualities born of prior practice-based associations. Second, although efforts to frame Nordic Walking in this way have been relatively successful, defining and classifying an emergent practice is not something that any one actor can control. As things turned out, Nordic Walking was initially associated with health and nature, as the promoters hoped, and soon after with specific categories of age and gender. These new connections arose as a consequence of the fact that middle-aged women were the first to take up the practice. As more and different people became involved, the social significance of participation and the meaning of Nordic Walking changed.

The dynamic relation between the status of participants and the meaning of the practices they carry is widely discussed, usually with the aim of understanding how social and cultural hierarchies are reproduced and sustained. By participating in some practices but not others, individuals locate themselves within society and in so doing simultaneously reproduce specific schemes and structures of meaning and order. In Bourdieu's terms, all cultural practices are 'automatically classified and classifying, rank ordered and rank ordering' (1984: 223). Writing in this tradition tends to emphasize the relative positioning not of the practice but of the practitioner within the social order. In other words, the interest is in what Nordic Walking says about the person who does it, not in how meanings like those of outdoor life circulate between practices or in how they combine with or break away from other symbolic constructs. By contrast, we want to put the element of meaning at the centre of our enquiry. One method of doing so is to think about how practices are classified and how categories themselves evolve. The business of sorting things and practices is politically significant, and it is this aspect that has attracted most attention (Bowker and Star, 2000a). But in the context of the present discussion the question is not 'Who determines whether smoking cigarettes and driving fast cars is transgressive or cool?', but rather, 'How are categories like those of being cool, healthy or youthful populated with practices, how does this population change and with what consequence for these frames of meaning?'.

One possibility is that meanings are extended and eroded as a result of dynamic processes of association. Accordingly, when Nordic Walking is linked with health, the meaning of wellbeing extends to encompass this practice, along with many others. The extension of one set of meanings sometimes implies the contraction of others. For example, concepts of 'freshness', conventionally associated with qualities of air, have found their way into the realm of laundering and bathing. As this 'new' element entered the practice of washing, other previously dominant themes of cleanliness or hygiene have been overlain, transformed or displaced. This is relevant in that notions of freshness legitimize and in a sense demand more frequent showering and laundering than ever before (Shove, 2003; Hand et al., 2005).

There are also instances in which meanings merge. In some circles, notions of youth and modernity are concurrently carried by practices like those of wearing jeans and leather jackets, and driving certain kinds of cars (O'Dell, 2001). Hebdige discusses similar processes of semiotic convergence in his article 'Towards a cartography of taste 1935–1961' (reproduced in Hebdige, 1988). His account of how 'ideologically charged connotational codes' intersected to constitute an 'Americanization' of taste is useful in showing that new meta-categories, like Americanization, can emerge through multiple conjunctions and can go on to have a life of their own. However, Hebdige's analysis concentrates on the consequences of such processes for social class distinctions and concepts of high and popular culture (in England), not on the details of intersection.

Since any one practitioner has limited first-hand experience of how a practice is reproduced by others, it is nearly always the case that elements of meaning are quite literally mediated. In Finland, representations and pictures of Nordic Walking in the press and on TV proved crucial in making key associations, for example, depicting Nordic Walkers in natural rather than urban settings, and illustrating other relevant features like the age and clothing of those involved. Infrastructures of mass communication are now such that there is virtually no limit to the settings through which such images might circulate. The catch is that while the media has a vital role in disseminating ideas, pictures and texts, there is no guarantee that these will stick. As with the abstraction and reversal of competence, the decoding and appropriation of meaning is an inherently local, inherently uncertain process. In addition, opportunities for association and re-classification are, to a degree, constrained and enabled by existing patterns and distributions of meaning.

The preceding paragraphs explored the possibility that what looks like the circulation and mutation of elements of meaning depends on successive, multi-sited, processes of de- and re-classification. This is what happens when concepts of freshness become important for the laundry, or when being healthy becomes linked to walking with 'sticks'. Similar processes are involved in the emergence and distribution of composite notions, including those of gender, youth and modernity. More abstractly, the classificatory texture of society changes as meanings merge and fragment, and although not the focus of this discussion, this ordering is important for questions of power (Bowker and Star, 2000a).

Packing and unpacking

We began this chapter by wondering about how the materials, competences and meanings of eating toast for breakfast circulate, and hence about how and where this might become (or remain) a normal thing to do. This led us to comment, element by element, on some of the routes and means of travel potentially involved. Rather than trying to provide a comprehensive catalogue of all possible forms of circulation we have picked on a few examples and used them to illustrate a handful of simple observations.

First, materials are the only elements that literally move in the sense of being physically transported. While competences and images appear to circulate, critical processes have to do with localized forms of de- and re-linking, a feature about which we have more to say below. Second, materials have characteristics (weight, fragility etc.) that affect, but which are only sometimes transformed by, processes of transportation. By contrast, meanings and competences are routinely modified as their reach and range extends or contracts. Third, with materials as with competences and meanings, the rate and extent of actual and potential circulation depends on the existence or otherwise of appropriate infrastructures, for instance, of transportation or mediation. Fourth, processes of codification and de-codification matter for the circulation of competence and mean-ing, but not for material. Fifth, some kinds of know-how can only be acquired and can only 'travel' if there is a base or foundation of existing competence on which to build. This limits the population of potential carriers and the extent to which specific competences can move. Sixth, acquiring new forms of skill often takes time. By contrast, meanings (i.e. forms of association) can change and emerge and can travel far and fast. That said, the effective appropriation of meanings and competences depends on local capacities to embed, 'reverse' and interpret. Such capacities are unevenly distributed and are, in turn, born of practices past.

Looking back at the *processes* involved we can identify similarities as well as differences in how elements travel. One striking feature is that movements of all forms routinely involve what we might think of as moments of packing and unpacking. This is quite literally the case for materials, and is metaphorically so for elements of meaning and compe-tence. Codification and abstraction, both forms of preparation, are often required. On arrival, the capacity to unpack – that is, to appropri-ate and decode – is correspondingly crucial and equally transformative. This is important in that processes of packing and unpacking are both defined and configured by local relations, histories and conditions. When in transit, and in so far as such a concept makes sense, elements might be momentarily free of such bonds, but there is no such independ-ent life for elements that are embedded in practice.

Although we have discussed them separately, competence, material and meaning are often so closely related that if one element should travel alone (abstracted and packed in isolation), it is likely to remain dormant until joined by others capable of bringing it into the frame of a living practice. This observation reminds us that relevant elements need to co-exist if prac-tices are to extend or endure. Having commented on how elements travel, we now turn to the ways in which they emerge, disappear and persist.

EMERGENCE, DISAPPEARANCE AND PERSISTENCE

In this section we explore the proposition that processes of emergence, persistence and disappearance are jointly involved in giving shape and form to the flow of elements with which, and in terms of which, we lead our lives.

Studies of innovation tend to focus on how new arrangements come into being and become established. This emphasis makes sense especially for businesses interested in building demand and developing and promoting profitable goods and services. However, if we focus on innovations in practice, making new links is almost certain to involve breaking previously important ties. Abernathy and Clark highlight this aspect in describing the impact of radical innovation. In their words:

> innovation of this sort disrupts and destroys. It changes the technology of process or product in a way that imposes requirements that the existing resources, skills and knowledge satisfy poorly or not at all. The effect is thus to reduce the value of existing competence, and in the extreme case, to render it obsolete.

> (Abernathy and Clark, 1985: 6)

In brief, the arrival of new elements may lead to, and may in fact depend on, the demise of others. Many examples of this kind involve the collapse of established skills and traditions in the face of technological innovation. As described in Chapter 2, the dynamics and pressures of motorized propulsion 'advanced and displaced the conventions of carriage makers' (Abernathy and Clark, 1985: 6). Other changes occur when established ways of thinking and working are overturned, as when dominant discourses crumble and paradigms shift (Kuhn, 1970). At a minimum, these observations suggest that emergence and disappearance are *related*, and that such processes are cumulatively important for the stocks of materials, competences and meanings in circulation at any one moment.

These stocks also depend on differential qualities of persistence and endurance. As we are about to see, certain elements can remain dormant, no longer part of any living practice, but still available for future use. Others are much more perishable. In describing some of these features, the next few paragraphs give a sense of how the lives of selected elements unfold over time, and how they weave together.

Our first sketch concerns the elements involved in writing with ink. The simple material story is essentially one of substitution: fountain pens displaced quills (during the 1880s) and were in turn upstaged by ball-points and biros (during the 1960s). Rather than focusing on this tale, we use this example to reflect on the characteristics of what we might think of as 'niches' not of innovation but of persistence. Fountain pens and ink are still available and in certain situations the skills involved – controlling the pen, managing ink, preventing leaks – are recurrently reproduced. Where people do use fountain pens, relevant materials and competences combine as closely as ever. Yet the symbolic significance of writing in ink is not as it was in the days when every school desk was equipped with an inkwell or when every child carried a pot of ink in his or her satchel. In short, the meaning and image of using an ink pen is relational, fluid and substantially transformed by the arrival and appro-priation of competing technologies. When many people defected to the biro, using a fountain pen became an unusual rather than a normal thing to do. The upshot is that while writing with ink survives, the meaning of the practice is not what it was. In this case, two elements (material, com-petence) are relatively stable but the third (meaning) is not. As in many other such instances, this transformation is directly related to the number of practitioners involved, a theme we develop in the next chapter.

For our second example we home-in on the relation between materi-als and competence. In organizing and scripting human and non-human actors, objects and infrastructures determine boundaries of competence, certain aspects being delegated to the technology, others remaining with the human. In some situations, materials stabilize and obdurately repro-duce know-how from the past, but in other cases the effect is the reverse. As we have seen, radical technological innovations can undermine the value of established skills and knock rival artefacts and systems out of the way. These processes are often linked. As things fall out of use, the know-how associated with them tends to disappear as well. Bit by bit, the reach of what was once common knowledge shrinks to the point that it becomes a little-known secret before vanishing sometimes, but not always without trace.

Records of past performance are occasionally preserved in the highly mediated form of written instruction. *Enquire Within Upon Everything: The great Victorian standby*, is a self-help guide published in 1856. It con-tains detailed advice on all manner of topics, including the production of

'Miscellaneous preparations'. Entry 2482, which is on making ink at home, runs as follows:

> For twelve gallons of ink take twelve pounds of bruised galls, five pounds of gum, five pounds of green sulphate of iron, and twelve gallons of rain-water. Boil the galls with nine gallons of the water for three hours, adding fresh water to supply that lost in vapour; let the decoction settle, and draw off the clear liquor. Add to it the gum, previously dissolved in one and a half gallons of water; dissolve the green vitriol separately in one and a half gallons of water, and mix the whole.

> (Philp, 1856)

The chances of anyone now wanting to make twelve gallons of ink at home are slim, but in theory, and assuming one could acquire the necessary ingredients, it would be possible to follow this recipe to the letter. But not all elements of competence are so easily preserved. Although the sequence is clearly described, it is possible that vital aspects of embodied learning and familiarity are missing from this unavoidably partial representation. Certain forms of competence, like the steps to be taken, have been stored and are now more widely available than ever before: the full text of *Enquire Within* can be found on the Internet. However, other aspects of embodied and tacit knowledge, like exactly how to draw off the clear liquor, have largely disappeared.

We have already discussed codification as an important moment in preparing and packing competence for 'travel'. It is now clear that knowledge that has been abstracted and codified occasionally persists in the reservoir long beyond the point at which it is routinely 'reversed' or enacted. Documents like *Enquire Within* contain and maintain knowledge that was once useful but which has become stranded in limbo as the capacity to decode (e.g. to understand what it is to draw off the liquor) has been eroded. Elements of skill can be preserved in different ways, but if they are to endure as fully functioning elements of practice, enactment is also required.

Our third example has to do with the persistence of meaning. In many respects meanings are the most delicate of the elements we consider: as we have already described, associations can be made, broken and appropriated really quickly (Hebdige, 1979).

In the previous section we suggested that meanings 'travel' as practices are grouped, re-grouped and categorized in different ways. When viewed from a temporal perspective, the idea that meanings are formed through multiple associations is a source of frailty and of strength. Take the concept of thrift. Not so long ago, practices that tapped into and sustained the category of thrift might include darning socks at home. Darning is now so rare that this link has broken. Faced with this minor set-back, notions of thrift have not diminished or lost their grip: instead they have moved on, becoming an important element of a range of other practices. As Gregson (2007) explains, being thrifty is now more likely to find expression in methods and styles of disposal and divestment than in repair. By implication, meanings move, mutate and take each other's place but are never preserved intact.

This does not mean that temporal sequences are of no significance, or that memories of what participation in specific practices once meant has no bearing on paths of future development. Adri de la Bruheze has written about the decline and resurgence of cycling as a means of transport in a range of European cities (de la Bruheze, 2000). During the 1940s, between 40 and 85 per cent of trips in the cities studied were made by bike and, for a time, cycling figured as an entirely 'normal' thing to do. In the 1970s there was a dramatic and sudden decline in rates of cycling across Europe. In England, where levels were especially low, cycling acquired a new image, becoming associated with leisure, masculinity and youth. It was no longer seen as part of daily life, nor was it classified as something that everyone would do.

Interestingly, rates of cycling have begun to increase, particularly in Denmark and the Netherlands, and in these locations, lost meanings of cycling as normal are being recovered. This is not so to anything like the same extent in the UK. In reflecting on why this might be the case, de la Bruheze speculates on the possibility that some symbolic (and also material) threshold might have been crossed, with the effect that cycling in British cities has fallen so far off the radar, and has been so strongly overlain by new connotations of leisure, that it struggles to be redefined as a normal means of transport. The other part of this argument is that in Denmark and the Netherlands, links with 'normality' could be reinstated because they had never fully vanished. We have more to say about these ideas in Chapter 8, 'Promoting transitions in practice', in which we discuss forms and means of policy intervention. For now the point is that even if meanings are not literally stored, sequences of de- and re-classification have an historical aspect that should not be overlooked.

In describing instances of emergence, disappearance and persistence we have noticed that relations between elements may vary as patterns of participation change. We have shown that material elements transform, carry and preserve forms of competence; that instructions are useful in keeping knowledge in circulation but that more is required to keep it alive; and that elements of meaning are capable of hopping from one practice to the next.

There is much more to be said about processes of accumulation and path dependence as these play out in different situations and with respect to different elements and combinations. Should we take such a discussion further we might explore parallels between the circulation and persistence of elements, and the individual and societal accumulation of what Bourdieu describes as different kinds of 'capital'. We might also identify ways of relating more conventional accounts of inequality and access to the historical and geographical distribution of materials, meanings and competences. These are tasks for the future. In this chapter we have established that such lines of enquiry are relevant and revealing. In the process we have shown that it can be useful to think of elements *as if* they had relatively autonomous trajectories amenable to analysis, interrogation and comparison. At the same time, it is clear that elements are nothing unless integrated in practice, and that if practices are to persist they need to recruit people willing and able to keep them alive.

RECRUITMENT, DEFECTION AND REPRODUCTION

Chapter 2 focused on making and breaking links between the elements of which practices are made. Chapter 3 concentrated on the lives of elements: on how they circulate, and on how they emerge, persist and disappear. This chapter is about the careers of individual practices and those who sustain them. Throughout we concentrate on practices-as-entities (rather than on practices-as-performances), and on people as 'body/minds who "carry" and "carry out" social practices' (Reckwitz, 2002: 256). Our central proposition is that the contours of *any one* practice – where is it reproduced, how consistently, for how long, and on what scale – depend on changing populations of more and less faithful carriers or practitioners. This generates a handful of related questions: how do practices attract recruits and how do they spread through social networks and communities? In more familiar terms, how do individuals initially encounter practices and then become their carriers? By following the careers of carriers as commitments develop and wane we get a sense of how some practices become more deeply anchored and embedded in society while others disappear. This is a key question and we end the chapter with a more concerted attempt to understand how 'dominant projects' become established (Pred, 1981).

For the most part we deal with relatively contemporary examples: How has showering become a normal thing to do? How did punk music emerge? Why did hula-hooping disappear? This makes sense in that each case tells us something different about how the careers of practitioners and practices intersect. Although it has its merits, this approach overlooks vital issues of history and inequality, both of which we touch on now.

We began by saying that the contours of *any one* practice depend on changing populations of more and less faithful carriers or practitioners. In theory, the same applies to the trajectories of *all* practices from the dawn of human history to the present. Taking the long view, we might therefore conclude that the range of practices in existence today results from an unbroken lineage of past patterns of persistence, transformation and disappearance. Just as the evolving ecology of Britain's forests can be traced back to the wild woods of the Mesolithic period, so the ancestry of contemporary practices might be traced through the habits of previous generations and the consequences these have had for accumulations of material and other resources. In woodland history, different species have taken hold, vanished, evolved and moved with changing patterns of climate, grazing and woodland management. About 8,500 BC, 'pine and hazel spread north, replacing birch which became uncommon for several thousand years' (Agate, 2005). More recent and more deliberate interventions in the form of coppicing, hedging, clearance and plantation have consequences of their own. All matter for the types of trees we see around us now.

The ecological analogy is useful in thinking about how practices mutate and change over time. It is also relevant when we change scale and, in a mind-boggling thought experiment, contemplate the totality of practices currently enacted on any one day around the world. If we ignore the possibility of multi-tasking, if we take the world population to be 6.8 billion, and if we take the practice of sleeping out of the equation (Harrison, 2009), each day affords something like 108 billion person-hours available to the many other practice-entities in circulation today. Which practices succeed in capturing these human resources? Which end up colonizing peoples' time and energy and which lose out? Equally important, what does the present ecology of practice mean for the future?

This is an intriguing way of thinking about social change, and one that evidently positions practices and not people centre stage, but as is immediately obvious there is no single global playing field across which all practices compete.

For a start, not every human being is capable of undertaking every possible practice, nor are practices uniformly distributed. In reality, the maximum number of person-hours a practice might capture is defined by the demands it makes and by existing distributions of relevant financial and material resources, physical ability, expertise and so on. In ecological terms, this argues for narrowing the scope of inquiry and concentrating on how practices grow and shrink within pockets or niches of possibility, remembering that these pockets change shape as practices develop.

That is one way to go, but we should perhaps turn the problem around. Rather than asking how social and material inequalities restrict the potential for one or another practice to develop, should we not also think about their impact on individual lives and the chances that people have? For Bourdieu, this is key. It is so in that the chances of becoming the carrier of any one practice are closely related to the social and symbolic significance of participation and to highly structured and vastly different opportunities to accumulate and amass the different types of capital required for, and typically generated by participation.

Whether framed from the point of view of practice or practitioner, inequities of access and participation are cumulative. In general terms, and again from both perspectives, past configurations are important for what might happen next. But in detail the timescales are often different. This is because the careers of practices-as-entities are defined by the performances of changing cohorts of carriers. Individuals are constantly taking up and dropping out of different practices as their lives unfold. Although this means that we can, and should, pay attention to issues of access and to how commitments change over an individual's life time, more is required to show how these combine to define the trajectories of practices-as-entities: trajectories that are, in turn and again in combination, relevant for future patterns of participation, experience and commitment.

More prosaically, the above discussion reminds us that the careers of practitioners and practices are intimately connected on a daily basis. Although this connection is theoretically convincing, it is inherently difficult to describe. If we are to write about actual and potential carriers we need to proceed as if the practices we discuss are stable, or at least stable enough for us to tell whether someone is involved in them or not. This is so even when the purpose of the discussion is to demonstrate the transformative effects of recruitment and defection. As in other chapters, we try to catch sight of these intersecting tracks by turning back and forth between the lives of practitioners and those of the practices they carry. This method allows us to 'talk about social relations in which persons and practices change, re-produce, and transform each other' (Lave and Wenger, 1991: 68). With this as our ambition, we start with a discussion of first encounters between emerging and existing practices and potential carriers.

FIRST ENCOUNTERS: NETWORKS AND COMMUNITIES

There are many reasons why individuals end up carrying specific practices. Accidents of birth, history and location are all important, as are social networks. Many of those who write about innovations in practice emphasize the significance of communities and networks as crucibles in which new arrangements are formed, as containers that limit their diffusion and as conduits through which they flow.

Nick Crossley's social network analysis of the handful of critical actors who were host to British punk's emerging form begins by focusing on the first of these possibilities. He argues that it was interaction within an already close-knit circle 'that generated punk' (Crossley, 2008: 94). As he goes on to explain, critical features, like the diameter of the circle and the density of links within it, proved to be important in allowing rapid interaction between members, establishing patterns of mutual obligation and enabling a productive concentration of energy and effort. The same arrangements that allowed punk practices to emerge also enabled them to take hold and diffuse. In effect the networks through which punk came into being, and through which its carriers were recruited, were formed by previous interests and affiliations. This suggests that new and emerging practices exploit connections forged and reproduced by practices that co-exist or that went before. Needless to say, these links are not randomly distributed, but in the case of punk, neither were they configured by intent.

In business and in industry, organizations have sought to bring 'communities of practice' into being by means of institutional design. The logic is simple. If close-knit networks are especially conducive to innovation, and if the diffusion of new practices mirrors movements of people within and between social worlds, why not arrange companies, cities and regions so that they facilitate these forms of interaction? The prospect of constructing and cultivating communities of practice, defined by Wenger and Snyder as 'groups of people informally bound together by shared expertise and passion for a joint enterprise' (2000: 139), is alluring but it seems that the capacity to bring such networks into being, and to do so with any degree of success, is typically limited.

One problem, discussed by Brown and Duguid (2001), is that the ties and connections through which practices develop and circulate, and by means of which they reach and capture new recruits, do not necessarily map onto organizational or institutional structures. Brown and Duguid's study of photocopy repair technicians illustrates this point. Their research showed that technicians who worked for different companies tended to have more in common with each other than with colleagues employed in other roles in their own firm (2001: 201). Whether they were aware of it or not, technicians in effect belonged to a cross-cutting community that had no formal organization but which had a texture and a structure that was itself important for how practices were reproduced and for how they changed. As with the punk circles described above, relevant bonds were formed through and as an outcome of previous and present experience.

In arguing that 'practices are ... the property of a kind of community created over time by the sustained pursuit of a shared enterprise' (Wenger, 1999: 45), Wenger takes these ideas a stage further, arriving at the conclusion that community and practice constitute each other. This is useful in explaining why top-down initiatives often run into trouble: if communities of practice are born of the experience of doing, they cannot be willed into existence or designed from afar. But it is also puzzling. If communities are defined by the practices in which members engage, can they also act as conduits through which practices flow?

One way out of this impasse is to notice that individuals engage in many practices and consequently belong to multiple communities at once. This insight is at the heart of methods like those of viral marketing. Since social networks overlap and extend beyond the margins of any one practice, they can be, and often are, important in generating what seem like chance encounters and unpredictable experiences. In our study of how Nordic Walking became established as a popular pastime we found that the practice spread by means of social contagion, moving between people who already knew each other as neighbours or as friends sharing other interests in common (Shove and Pantzar, 2005). This is not at all unusual. As with the diffusion of punk, new recruits were drawn into the scene through established networks.

So far we have underlined the relevance of existing social ties (themselves outcomes of existing or past practices) for the formation and diffusion of new ways of walking and of making music. However, this is not the whole story. Practices that survive for more than a generation need to attract fresh cohorts of carriers to replace those who defect or die. As our next example shows, modes of recruitment take different forms as practices become established.

In many Western societies, daily showering has captured so many loyal followers that participation no longer indicates membership of one or another social group, nor are such networks relevant for its diffusion. By implication, rates of penetration matter for how people are captured. Where practices are widespread within any one group or society, the chances of encounter are that much higher. And in situations where participation is simply expected, recruitment follows as a matter of course. There are, in addition, instances in which people are required to adopt or refrain from certain practices by law.

There are no laws about showering on a daily basis but the practice has become embedded through material and not only social networks. As a result, people are in a sense recruited to showering by the design of the bathroom and the products on sale, as well as by the expectations of friends and family (Burke, 1996). Much the same applies to driving. In cities planned around the car, it is often difficult to move around in other ways. In sum, and in brief, channels of recruitment change as the careers of individuals, practices and related infrastructures and institutions develop. First encounters are surely critical, but where participation is in any sense voluntary more is required if practices are to retain faithful cohorts of suitably committed carriers.

CAPTURE AND COMMITMENT: CAREERS AND CARRIERS

How are practices shared and transmitted from one carrier to the next? Lizardo (2009) and Turner (2001) are both concerned with the philosophical challenges that sharing presents for theories of practice. For Turner, 'the idea that there are shared practices requires some sort of notion of how they come to be shared, and this notion in turn dictates how practices can be conceived' (2001: 120). For Lizardo and Strand (2010), this is a significant problem in that practical knowledge – that is, knowledge of doing – is born of first-hand, embodied experience and does not live in the realm of discursive consciousness.

The fact that many forms of knowing are involved, some tacit, some explicit, has not prevented sociologists from describing *how* new recruits are initiated into practices as varied as those of getting drunk (MacAndrew and Edgerton, 1969), giving up drinking (Cain, 1991), having sex (Gagnon and Simon, 1974), repairing photocopiers (Suchman, 1984) or serving cocktails (Spradley and Mann, 1975). These accounts, typically written from the point of view of the novice practitioner, document the exchange and acquisition of practical know-how. They show

how procedural knowledge is absorbed through processes of 'mimetic apprenticeship' (Lizardo, 2009: 9), they explain the importance of material artefacts (tools, infrastructures), and they document the significance of sequence, time and timing.

In going beyond the realm of explicit instruction and the inculcation of attitudes and values, these analyses of situated learning are consistent with Turner's interpretation of practices as 'lessons that enable them [people] to do particular things such as go to the beach and be comfortable with the responses of other people' (2001: 130). Sociological representations of induction frequently allow us to see how lessons of this type are shared. Many go on to characterize the dynamic relation between the practitioner and the practice in which he or she is engaged, demonstrating that processes of sharing and learning are transformative, both of the practitioner and the practice in which they are engaged.

It is in this context that the notion of a career comes into its own. In the world of work, careers consist of recognized stages through which individuals pass as they climb the occupational ladder. Starting off as newcomers, their status changes each time they reach another rung. In *Asylums*, Goffman uses concepts of progression and changing status to describe the moral career of mental patients as they take on the roles expected of them as inmates in a total institution (Goffman, 1975 [1961]). Howard Becker does much the same in *Outsiders*, a classic study of how people become marijuana users and jazz musicians (1963). In this book Becker shows how experiences, expertise and identities evolve as new recruits learn the ropes and as they become enmeshed in existing communities of practice. Starting off as 'outsiders', novices are drawn into and simultaneously defined by the practices in which they engage, or by which they are caught. As their careers develop, participants see themselves and are seen by others in a different way. In the situations Becker describes there is a point somewhere along the line at which people who have been taking drugs define themselves as 'drug-takers' and as fully-fledged members of a community in which this is a normal and not a deviant thing to do.

As people become committed to the practices they carry, their status changes sometimes to the point that they *become* that which they do (Becker, 1977). The practicalities of becoming what Lave and Wenger

(1991) refer to as a 'full practitioner' and the sequences and stages involved vary from one practice to another. This is relevant in that at any one moment, a practice will be populated and carried by people with different degrees of experience and commitment. Needless to say, some drop out along the way.

For individual practitioners, defection and continued participation are often in tension. The nature of this tension changes as critical thresholds are passed. As indicated above, the moment when someone sees him or herself *as* a doctor or drug-taker may prove to be a moment of no-return: from that point on, their career is set. More commonly, repeated performances bind practitioners and practices together in many more subtle ways. Regular trips to the gym have a noticeable effect on the muscles, strength and shape of those who devote themselves to body-building (Crossley, 2006). And with body-builders, as with home-improvement enthusiasts (Watson and Shove, 2008), bird watchers (Hui, 2011) and amateur jazz pianists (Sudnow, 1993), new levels of practice come within reach as competence develops.

So far we have commented on the routes through which individuals become committed carriers. Let us now switch perspective and ask what these processes mean for the careers of the practices themselves. At any one moment, 'a practice' consists of a composite patchwork of variously skilled, variously committed performances enacted and reproduced by beginners and by old-hands alike. Patterns of career development are, in combination, relevant for the trajectory of the practice as a whole. This is so in that newcomers and those with more experience inevitably reproduce somewhat different variants.

Lave and Wenger describe conflicts that arise as novices become old-timers and as 'the forces that support processes of learning' rub up against 'those that work against them' (Lave and Wenger, 1991: 57). There is a tendency, particularly in writing which focuses on induction and apprenticeship, to suppose that new generations, still at the periphery, have greater scope and motivation for doing things differently and that old-hands, who define the core, are typically stuck in their ways. This is not always so, as Franke and Shah (2003) discovered in their investigation of innovation in a range of extreme sports. With canyoning as with sail planing, definitions of skilled performance proved to be more fluid, dynamic and emergent amongst those with greatest experience. In these examples the most committed practitioners were also the most unfaithful. In the worlds that Franke and Shah describe, new tricks and techniques arose from the embodied experience of participation and were shared, in the first instance, between sub-sets of devoted practitioners whose performances constantly redefined the practice's leading edge.

In these situations experienced practitioners define career paths that others then follow. In other settings it is novices who bring new ways of doing into being. In both cases the ways in which relations between newcomers and old-hands are structured is critical for the circulation (or not) of expertise and for how careers develop. Lave and Wenger describe the social and political organization of different pathways to full participation in some detail. Butchery is one of the examples they consider. In the organizations they observed, meat-cutting tasks requiring different levels of expertise were clearly demarcated and allocated in terms of a well-defined hierarchy. Apprentices were set to work on simple jobs but had no sense of the complexities of butchery that lay ahead. They only discovered what the next stages involved as they climbed the ladder, rung by rung. By comparison, trainee midwives acquired a better sense of what full participation entailed right from the start. In documenting these arrangements and in noticing that apprentices often learn as much from each other as from their 'masters', Lave and Wenger conclude that 'mastery resides not in the master but in the organization of the community of practice of which the master is a part' (1991: 94).

This begs further questions about how communities come to be structured as they are. Outside the realm of formal organization, and sometimes within it too, evolving practices routinely change the margins of relevant networks and the scope of who they do and do not include. As snowboarders split away from skiers, new communities of practice formed. Similarly, when practices diffuse through social hierarchies, for instance as people emulate those of higher status, the meaning of participation changes: an influx of new recruits often leads to the exit of others. These dynamics matter for the number of people involved at any one time. In addition, the relation between the core and the periphery (i.e. between full participants and novices) is crucial for the generation of variety and for how practices change from within. However, not all practices are reproduced by identifiable communities, nor are all characterized by pathways of career progression.

Again, showering is a good example. Over the last century the number of people who regularly take a shower has increased dramatically. When interviewed about what showering involves, respondents generally claim to be set in their ways: showering is something they do day-in, day-out and without thought or innovation (Hand et al., 2005). Unlike some of the sports considered above, this practice is not obviously transformed by enthusiastic lead users, nor is there a tradition that novices are tempted to overthrow. No one seems to be changing what it is to take a shower, but national and international data on the water used for personal hygiene demonstrate that the timing of the experience, the force of the flow and the valuing of freshness and invigoration are on the move (Walker, 2009). Daily showering, viewed as a totality, is being reconfigured by subtle but cumulative differences in the elements of which it is formed, including plumbing technologies and products, and in how these are integrated by its many carriers, all of whom take their routine to be *the* normal thing to do. In other words, practices like showering can and do emerge and evolve through multiple minor adjustments made in private but made possible by the circulation of new and different materials, meanings and forms of competence.

There are many possible routes of capture, commitment and change, and we have only described a few. These few nonetheless indicate that learning, sharing and carrying are typically and perhaps unavoidably transformative, both of the practitioners involved and of the practices they reproduce. This conclusion puts issues of access and engagement in a new light. Patterns of participation matter not only for who gets the opportunity to do what, but for who it is that shapes the future of a practice, and for how individuals are shaped by the experience. All are significant for accumulations of expertise, for the meaning of participation and for the distribution of requisite materials: in short, for the production of future possible trajectories, individual and collective. These are important conclusions, but they are also conclusions derived from relatively tame examples of incremental change. In the next section we discuss somewhat more dramatic instances of radical transformation, mass defection and almost total collapse.

COLLAPSE AND TRANSFORMATION: THE DYNAMICS OF DEFECTION

Schatzki suggests that judgements about whether practices have died or merely been transformed should reflect the extent and character of change. He provides the following guidance: 'where multiple mutations are accompanied by continuities in other components, a practice lives on', but 'when changes in organization are vast or wholesale, or a practice's projects and tasks are simply no longer carried out, former practices expire' (2002: 244).

Expiration can be an outcome of radical transformation, a consequence of mass defection, or both. In a recent analysis of differences between innovations, fashions and fads, Gronow (2009) describes a range of possibilities. He argues that innovations generate lasting change in routines and habits. To the extent that this is so, innovations entail extinction: old ways are abandoned as new ones are adopted. Fashions are different in that they are characterized by cyclical processes of substitution: last year's model is replaced by this year's design, but in the end and at the level of practice, nothing really changes. 'Despite its novelty a new fashion does not change any social habits' (Gronow, 2009: 134). Finally, fads spring up and then simply die. Unlike innovations, there is nothing waiting in the wings to take their place. We use this scheme to discuss the different forms of defection involved, starting with fads.

Meyersohn and Katz contend that 'The study of fads and fashions may serve the student of social change much as the study of fruit flies has served geneticists: neither the sociologist nor the geneticist has to wait long for a new generation to arrive' (1957: 594). We are not interested in fads for this reason, for their significance as expressions of crowd psychology (Meyersohn and Katz, 1957) or as moments in cycles of distinction and identification (Simmel, 1957). For us their value lies in the clues they provide as to how massively popular practices suddenly lose their grip. Hula-hooping is a fine example. In the late 1950s, 25 million hula hoops were sold in two months with 100 million international orders following soon after (Knerr, 1997). Two years later the craze had largely passed. So how come so many new recruits gave up so fast? We consider three possible explanations, all relevant for a broader discussion of defection.

The first has to do with the extent and character of what MacIntyre describes as 'internal rewards' (MacIntyre, 1985). In brief, the idea is that performing a practice well, that is in terms of standards that are part and parcel of the definition of a practice itself, is of immediate, internal reward. For example, being an excellent teacher is satisfying in and of itself and not (only) because this role attracts public recognition or a good salary, these being external rather than internal rewards. There are certainly some for whom hula-hooping is, in these terms, internally rewarding. However, hula-hooping's brief career might suggest that self-propelling circuits of satisfaction were limited, or distinctly short-lived. Compared with long-standing leisure pursuits like gardening, home improvement or cooking, all fields in which expertise accumulates through sequences of variously successful accomplishment and in which one project often begets another, hula-hooping appears a little thin. Though capable of retaining a handful of enthusiasts, it seems that the experience was not of itself enough to generate lasting interest nor the reward sufficient to sustain the commitment of the 125 million or more who gave hula-hooping a go. To put this observation the other way around, practices are, perhaps ironically, better able to retain commitment when they afford scope for innovation.

A second possibility is that hula-hooping disappeared as rapidly as it arrived because it had no symbolic or normative anchoring: it was not strongly associated with either good or bad behaviour, with the reproduction of distinctions, or with fulfilling injunctions and obligations. Exactly which practices fall into the 'must do' category and exactly how layers of symbolic meaning are lost and acquired differs widely, but at any one moment daily lives are organized by sets of seemingly unavoidable commitments (Douglas, 1984; Kaufmann, 1998). Since fads like swinging a ring of plastic around the hips are of no wider significance, defection is easy. A third related point is that hula-hooping was not obviously connected to and not obviously dependent on any other practice: it came into being, existed briefly and then died alone.

These interpretations suggest that mass defection is possible, and perhaps even likely, where practices are not consistently internally rewarding, not laden with symbolic significance and not enmeshed in wider networks.

However, there are many exceptions. Routinely cycling to work is one. In the early 1950s in the UK, around 40 per cent of journeys to work were by bike. In less than twenty years this dropped to just a few per cent (Pooley and Turnbull, 2000). In thinking about how cycling lost so many carriers in such a few years we need to think about how practices fit together. Cycling to work was, for a while, deeply embedded in a whole set of social and institutional arrangements. Rather than constituting a form of enduring strength, this interdependence was a source of weakness: the entire cycle-based regime caved in as automobility took hold. One by one, hundreds and thousands of previously committed cyclists abandoned this mode of travel and in so doing reinforced the dominance of the car.

In Gronow's terms, cycling is not a fad: though it disappeared fast, it did so in relation to an incoming innovation. In everyday terms this is but one example of an entirely familiar process in which old ways are abandoned as new ones become established. Moral and ideological changes have similar effect: ruling out and in some cases outlawing arrangements that were once taken for granted, and sometimes doing so in ways that affect many practices at once. More straightforwardly, letting go is part of moving on.

But again this is not the whole story. Although there is some merit in thinking about how hours are allocated, and although it is true that (multi-tasking aside) time spent on one practice is not devoted to another, defection and recruitment are not simply two sides of the same coin. As illustrated by the dynamic relation between Internet use and meanings of family life, social and technical innovation is not just a matter of swapping one cohort of carriers for another. In its first five years the Internet managed to capture an average of 10 hours a week from around 50 per cent of the population of the USA (Nie, 2001: 430). In wondering about where these 201,017,857 hours (based on 2001 figures) had come from, commentators worried that the Internet was stealing time previously spent with friends and family (Kraut et al., 1998: 1031). Early surveys suggested that this might be so. However, more detailed analyses demonstrated that time spent on the computer is routinely defined and configured by multiple coexisting practices, including those through which bonds of friendship and family are maintained (Slater, 2003). Rather than taking time away, the Internet appears to be changing what it is to do family and friendship and modifying the practices involved. Some kinds of defection are involved, but the process is not one of replacement or simple competition.

It might be possible to identify features typical of a fad, or to anticipate the kinds of collapse associated with radical innovation, one practice at a time. But as is already obvious, the margins of a practice, its ability to capture and retain recruits and prevent them from defecting depend on its positioning in a sea of other practices, each with relatively volatile, relatively static trajectories of their own. This argues for thinking about the relation between recruitment, defection and reproduction on a societal scale.

Again this is a mind-boggling suggestion, but what if there were some means of assessing the rates at which individual practices are changing, and hence the relative 'plasticity or rigidity (lock-in) of the interlocking systems of practice of which society is composed' (Shove, 2009: 30)? During the course of any one day, individuals devote time and attention to an immense variety of practices by which they are captured. Some of these are on the way in, others are on the way out. Some are stable, others are mutating fast. Should such a thing as a societal index of practice transformation exist, it might indicate that certain domains of daily life are moving more quickly, or are more dynamic than others. It might show that some such changes are necessarily synchronized, or cumulative, and that others are not. As they go about their daily lives, people are unknowingly engaged in reproducing and enacting multiple and varied cycles of change, simultaneously shaping the lives of practices and being shaped by them.

In the last part of this chapter we elaborate on the relation between what Allan Pred (1981) describes as the daily paths and life paths of individuals and the practices and dominant projects they carry. This allows us to show how patterns of recruitment and defection play out over the longer run.

DAILY PATHS, LIFE PATHS AND DOMINANT PROJECTS

This far we have argued that practices-as-entities expand, contract and change as they acquire and lose variously faithful cohorts of carriers.

Their capacity to attract recruits depends in part on the distribution of relevant elements (Chapter 3), on their position with respect to other practices and on the characteristics of the social networks through which they circulate, and which they also constitute. When considered from the point of view of the individuals involved, these same processes relate to experiences like those of joining or leaving different communities of practice; mobilizing (or not mobilizing) requisite elements and acquiring (or losing) relevant forms of commitment, capacity and experience.

If we were to home-in on the life of any one practice, or any one individual, we would need to add more detail. For example, practices that can only be carried by those who are fit and healthy, who are of teenage years, or who already have certain skills or wealth, recruit from already limited populations. If they are to survive for any length of time, extremely demanding sports need to secure a steady stream of future carriers willing to take over from those whose careers end after a year or two of devoted commitment. Similarly, but this time from the practitioner's point of view, it is usual to take up and abandon different pursuits as one moves through the life course. Defection is inevitable as childish ways are put aside, as new loves are found and as bodies gain and lose strength and agility.

Although the temporal scales are often different, the life paths of individual carriers intersect with, and in aggregate constitute the life paths of individual practices. This makes sense, but something more is required if we are to understand how processes of accumulation play out during an individual lifetime and across the lifetimes of the practices that are carried.

We have so far used the concept of career to describe the ways in which commitments build, but another important feature is that taking one path and not another configures opportunities for the future. Having children, changing occupations or moving to another country all have such effect. When people move into (or are captured by) institutional roles, the details of their day – in Pred's terms, their daily path – are structured by projects and priorities that are of consequence for the 'accretion of competences and dispositions' (Pred, 1981: 14) and hence for their life path as a whole. In this analysis, not all practices are equal. Instead, lives revolve around a handful of 'dominant projects', these being inter-linked practices that in combination 'require that participating individuals expend their labour power or in some other way engage themselves in activity in a given manner, at a given time and place' (1981: 16).

Dominant projects are influential on several fronts at once. In concentrating priorities and energies they focus time and attention in some directions and not others. This has consequences for the skills and expectations that develop as a result. By these means, individuals' lives are woven into the reproduction of dominant societal institutions. To quote Pred again:

> [I]nstitutions occupying positions of societal domination are those whose projects are dominant either in the sense that they take time-allocation and scheduling precedence over both the projects of other institutions and extra-institutionally individually defined projects, or in the sense that the time resources they demand force some other projects to be pushed aside totally and obliterated along with any traditional skills and knowledge necessary to their performance.
>
> (Pred, 1981: 16)

In this chapter we have given a partial sense of how this ebb and flow works out, from first encounters between novices and emerging or established practices through to forms of commitment and defection. But we need to do more if we are to show how certain practices rise to dominance and how others are marginalized. These are themes explored in Chapter 5.

CONNECTIONS
BETWEEN PRACTICES

Chapter 2, 'Making and breaking links', explored the proposition that practices emerge, persist and disappear as links between their defining elements are made and broken. Chapter 3, 'The life of elements', focused on the ways in which materials, meanings and competences circulate and endure. Chapter 4, 'Recruitment, defection and reproduction', dealt with the careers of practices and of those who carry them. This chapter is about how practices relate to each other.

Just as elements are linked together to form recognizable practices, so practices link, one to another, to form bundles and complexes. Bundles are loose-knit patterns based on the co-location and co-existence of practices. Complexes represent stickier and more integrated combinations, some so dense that they constitute new entities in their own right. Inter-practice relations of these and other kinds have emergent, cumulative and often irreversible effects for individual practices, for the elements of which they are composed, and for the spatial and temporal texture of daily life. That much is clear, but what of the detail? How are these linkages most usefully conceptualized? In this chapter we consider various strategies consistent with our own deliberately slim-line version of practice theory.

So far we have been working with the proposition that practices involve the active integration of elements (materials, meanings, competences) and that through these integrative performances practices are reproduced as provisionally recognizable entities. In keeping with this strategy, we have taken practices to be whatever actual and potential practitioners recognize as such. This is important for how we approach the task of characterizing relations between practices.

Since our model consists simply of elements, practices, practitioner-carriers and connections between them, we do not work with distinctions that are important for others. For instance, we have not concerned ourselves with differences between what Schatzki describes as 'dispersed' practices like writing or following rules, and more complex 'integrative' practices including cooking, farming or weaving (Schatzki, 1996: 98). Nor have we sought to discriminate, as Schatzki does, between doings, sayings, activities, tasks and projects on the one hand, and practices on the other. In Schatzki's terms, a practice 'embraces a set of hierarchically organized doings/sayings, tasks and projects' (2002: 73): for us it is a necessarily provisional, but relatively consistent, relatively enduring integration of elements.

By holding fast to this approach we are able to describe historically fluid processes of linkage, disruption and mutual influence and identify instances in which practices become so closely connected that distinctions between them dissolve. Driving, as discussed in Chapter 2, is a good example. When cars were first introduced, keeping them in motion depended on a series of linked but discrete practices, each involving distinctive combinations of meanings, materials and competence, and each having a history of its own. Signalling and overtaking drew on skills of horse-riding, and starting the car engine was a mechanical operation in its own right. Over the last century component practices have merged such that driving is now recognized and enacted as a single entity. When teaching novices how to drive, instructors may break the total performance down into different moves, each treated and experienced as a separate practice by the learner-driver and by the instructor alike, but only for a while. The common aim is for the recruit to seam-lessly integrate these procedures so as to reproduce what is now known as 'driving'. In the language of science and technology studies, driving has been 'black-boxed' to the extent that it constitutes a single practice.

Not all forms of inter-practice connection result in the emergence of new hybrid entities. Concepts like those of lifestyle or habitus describe looser collections of what remain evidently separate pursuits, including eating, drinking, holidaying, reading and television viewing. There are, in addition, many other ways in which practices restrict, enable and condition each other. As we have already noticed, new practices often take hold at the expense of others which are no longer performed, or not performed as frequently as before. Some also act as dominant forces resulting in and perpetuating distinctive concentrations and accumula-tions of human and other resources, and consequently shaping path-ways of future development. The purpose of this chapter is to explore how practices are connected and how they shape each other. In thinking about relations between practices, we begin by imagining three basic formulations: one in which practices exist but without being integrated, one in which practices are provisionally linked by ties of co-existence or co-dependence, and one in which connections are no longer sustained. Figure 5.1 illustrates these abstract possibilities.

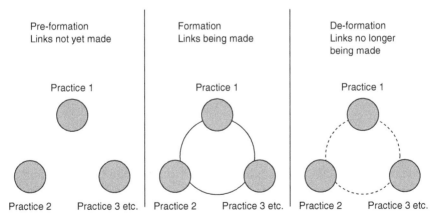

Figure 5.1 The pre-formation, formation and de-formation of connections between practices

Like practices themselves (see Chapter 2), relations between practices require ongoing reproduction if they are to persist for any length of time. While some connections are obvious to those involved in keeping them alive, others are not: accordingly, practices can and do co-exist and co-depend in ways that their practitioner-carriers barely recognize. If we are to describe relations between practices we need to characterize the types of linkage involved, the processes through which such bonds are formed, and the ways in which dominant projects and systems emerge. We make a start by showing how practices come together in space and time.

BUNDLES AND COMPLEXES

Practices that are routinely enacted in similar places, for instance in kitchens, bathrooms or offices, are not necessarily connected by virtue of co-location alone. However, there are various ways in which spatial arrangements constitute and underpin potentially important patterns of association. Some have to do with the physical location of material elements. For example, practices requiring good supplies of running water converge around taps and drains. In effect, plumbing infrastructures bring practices together in ways that allow, but do not ensure, their mutual influence (Muthesius, 1982). Shared elements of meaning can work in much the same way. For instance, concepts of privacy and propriety are important for what happens where, and hence for the range of practices likely to be reproduced in any one space.

Since buildings represent sites in which practices are contained, separated and combined, the history of domestic architecture provides a telling record of how daily life is organized and how this changes. In suburban homes built a century or so ago, eating generally took place in the dining room and cooking in the kitchen. There are various reasons why this formal separation is no longer so strict and why kitchendiners have come into vogue – these include changing gender relations, systems of provision and conventions of family life. For present purposes, the more important point is that open kitchens enable closer associations not only between cooking and eating but also between pre-paring food and socializing (Cieraad, 2002). It is impossible to tell whether these novel conjunctions will be of lasting significance for the trajectories of any of the practices involved, but the potential is there. As our next example shows, relatively loose connections, initially born of co-location, can prove relevant for the course of social and institutional change.

In their analysis of the office as an innovation junction, De Wit et al. (2002) underline the importance of spatial and material arrangements for the re-structuring of administrative practice. Their historical account of the development of office technology emphasizes the coordinative role of the typewriter. This device, together with carbon paper, permitted the emergence of a new practice (typing) in which writing and copying combined. Typing was in turn important for the flow of paper and for the development and institutionalization of other tasks like those of filing and storing. In effect, the typewriter 'became the centre of an administrative organization in which the technologies employed in producing, reproducing and storing documents were increasingly linked' (De Wit et al., 2002: 58). As these authors explain, the office setting proved crucial for the detail of how typing, copying and organizing merged to produce new divisions of administrative labour. Individual firms responded differently, and not all offices are the same. It is nonetheless clear that 'the office' had a coordinative and transformative role not (or not only) as an exact location but as a generic environment facilitating equally generic linkages, ultimately resulting in the transformation of office life itself. As this case indicates, sites like offices and homes can have emergent consequences for the trajectories of individual practices and hence for the collection of practices that are, and that are not, enacted in such environments.

More broadly, the idea that co-location might be important in facilitating innovation has attracted much attention and has done so at many scales including that of the city and the region. For writers like Amin and Thrift, the vibrancy of world cities and the opportunities they afford for spontaneity and surprise are directly related to the density and variety of practices enacted within them. Developing this theme, they analyse the urban as a 'force field' or coordinative node facilitating the intersection and the flow of moralities, cultures, economic resources, knowledge, power and relations of trust (Amin and Thrift, 2007). In this literature, proximity is taken to be important because it increases the chances of cross-fertilization between otherwise unrelated practices.

Practices reproduced in homes, offices and cities condition each other in different ways and with varied consequences. Some interactions result in mutual adaptation, others in destruction, synergy or radical transformation. Although important, these are not the only routes through which practices connect. As we are about to see, temporal relationships of sequence and synchronization are also vital.

Hutchins (1995) provides a brilliantly detailed description of the coordinative work involved in gently easing a massive ship into dock. As he explains, the intensely choreographed business of bringing tonnes of steel to rest at exactly the right spot requires the careful synchronization of many separate practices. As the process of docking proceeds, relations of co-dependence are tangible and real. Complex operations of this kind depend on the efficient and effective sequencing of multiple practices (some have to come before others), on smooth processes of hand-over and on the capacity for rapid mutual adjustment and synchronized adaptation as circumstances change (some practices have to happen at the same time).

In situations like these it is almost impossible to distinguish between the spatial and temporal aspects of inter-practice coordination. Nor does it make sense to separate the performance of the many practices involved from the institutional and infrastructural systems in which they are embedded/of which they are constituted. For example, within hospitals, buildings are (usually) designed to allow speedy interaction in emergency situations. And within any one of these spaces, layouts are configured such that the tools required by different but co-dependent specialists are all to hand. In other words, the anticipated intersection of working practices constitutes a kind of meta system in terms of which individual practices (and elements) are oriented.

As Zerubavel's (1979) analysis of patterns of time in hospital life demonstrates, there are many levels at which practices come together and many temporal rhythms involved. It is true that the timing of a medical procedure depends, in part, on the patient's condition, but it also depends on patterns of shift-work, the day of the week and the time of the year, all of which are relevant for the scheduling and coordination of parallel practices including those of training junior staff, keeping the administration running and managing the flow of work. Within hospitals as within other areas of daily life any one practice cuts into and cuts through multiple registers of interaction, often figuring in several overlapping sequences and cycles at once. Sometimes merely co-existing, sometimes co-depending, the resulting patterns of cross-practice connection are inextricably interwoven.

This discussion of the sites and settings in which practices shape each other indicates that practice *bundles*, by which we mean loose-knit patterns like those based on co-location, sometimes turn into stickier forms of co-dependence. This does not always happen, and there are many instances in which practices co-exist without troubling one another at all. But when practices do come to depend upon each other (whether in terms of sequence, synchronization, proximity or necessary co-existence), they constitute *complexes*, the emergent characteristics of which cannot be reduced to the individual practices of which they are composed. This is all very well, but there is surely more to say about why inter-practice relations take the form they do and about how complexes and bundles are made and broken.

COLLABORATION AND COMPETITION

Pantzar and Sundell-Nieminen (2003) talk about an 'ecology of goods' within the home and go on to describe 'predatory' relations between a digital camera and its analogue 'prey', contrasting these with mutually supportive arrangements like those between a computer and associated furniture including shelves and chairs. Can similar ideas be used to understand and characterize relations between practices? We have already made quite some moves in this direction. In Chapter 4, 'Recruitment, defection and reproduction', we explored the possibility that practices compete with each other for recruits and carriers. Elsewhere we argued that their survival depends on the existence of requisite materials, meanings and forms of competence, and on their capacity to capture these resources (Chapter 3, 'The life of elements'). In this section we explore the suggestion that bundles and complexes arise and disappear as a consequence of competition and/or collaboration between practices.

As described above, certain practices (docking a ship, conducting a surgical operation) suppose and require the reproduction of others. For example, oil-tanker captains depend on harbours and docks and on global networks of people capable of faithfully reproducing docking practices when called upon to do so. In cases where sequences are important, and where one practice produces elements (for example, competences or materials) on which another depends, pre- and co-requisite practices 'collaborate' in the reproduction of more extensive complexes in which all have a part to play.

Not all chains of interdependence are symmetrical and relatively 'flat' examples of mutual support exist alongside other more complex hierarchies. For example, in the world of organized sports, national and international leagues depend on players and local clubs willing and able to enter higher level competitions. The benefits probably flow in both directions: local clubs certainly gain from interest generated at the international level, but at the end of the day, international forms could not exist without the grass roots versions. In this situation, one set of practices sustains another but the balance of power is unequal. Whilst practices arguably compete for elements, they are also united by those they have in common. For example, material innovations like the Sony Walkman linked otherwise unrelated practices such as going for a run or doing the housework and listening to music (Weber, 2005). Although impressive, the coordinative potential of the Walkman is as nothing compared to that now offered by laptops and smart phones capable of bridging between entertainment (games, watching TV/DVD); socializing (Skype, email, Facebook); household management (online banking); learning and working (Røpke, 2001). Meanings and concepts like those of freshness or Westernization have a similarly coordinative role, providing a common point of reference for disparate pursuits. As we saw in Chapter 3, drinking, driving and wearing jeans became associated with each other, each reproducing and at the same time being reproduced by cross-cutting images of modernity and youth (O'Dell, 2001). In these ways, shared elements sustain and are sustained by forms of cross-practice 'collaboration', broadly defined.

There are surely other forms of mutual support but in describing these few we give a sense of the potential for sharing and integration and the terms on which this might be based. What then of competition? How do practices compete with each other, and how do the outcomes of such contests affect the spatial and temporal ordering of daily life and the bundles and complexes of which it is composed?

In the previous chapter we referred to a seemingly competitive relationship between the Internet and family life. While some commentators worried about computers stealing time from friends and family, others argued rather than being undermined by this technology such relations were, instead, mediated by it. As this debate suggests, it is not always easy to tell whether relations between practices are competitive (such that the Internet erodes family life) or collaborative (such that the Internet strengthens family ties). In this case, knowing how much time people spend glued to the computer is not particularly informative. However, there are instances in which time-use data reveals what seem to be aggressively competitive moves in which one practice colonizes resources and captures recruits at the expense of another.

Time use studies from the 1950s onwards show that the arrival of the television has transformed both the sequencing and the character of other leisure pursuits. In the early days this was not a foregone conclusion. Griffiths and Holden refer to a newspaper article (*Daily Sketch*, 14 April 1952) which indicates that gardening was, at the time, holding its own:

> Many people will watch television this afternoon and evening instead of going out. There will be few gardeners among them however. A BBC inquiry into the changes TV makes in family life reveals that it is seldom allowed to come between a man and his flowerbeds.
>
> (Griffith and Holden, 2004: 1)

Gardening remains extremely popular but audience figures demonstrate that television has gained ground and that flowerbeds have lost the prime-time commitment they once commanded.

With the television, as with the Internet, the ecological metaphor needs to be taken further if it is to be of value. Up to a point, it may be useful to think of practices collaborating and competing for resources and attention. However, simple representations of this kind overlook the more subtle point that the recurrent enactment of practices and of links between them transforms the terms in which competition and/or collaboration are framed. Put differently, bundles and complexes of practice are implicated in the reproduction of space and time and the distribution of requisite elements (material, meaning and competence). Other studies of television viewing give a sense of what more is involved.

On average, people spend more time watching television now than they did ten or even five years ago, but to understand what this means for changing relations between practices, we need to know more about how these minutes are allocated, and about the details and dynamics of sequence and timing. Within any one home, evening meals are variously planned to coincide with a favourite programme, or to allow those partaking of them the opportunity to eat together, or to eat and then go out and so on. Each scenario involves an interweaving of different practices (eating, viewing television, interacting, gardening etc.) that in combination define a specific pattern of daily life. While there is enormous individual variation in when and how television watching takes place, this juggling is anything but random (Silverstone, 1993). The now well-established concept of prime time – the time when audience figures are highest – consequently emerges as an outcome of collective and dynamic 'negotiation' between television programmers and millions of different households. Having become established, prime time in turn affects other kinds of domestic scheduling. The resulting re-arrangements are not simply outcomes of competition, but are instead collectively implicated in changing the terms on and the times in which practices vie with each other for attention.

More abstractly, interpretations of possible, potential and proper time and timing are critical for the ongoing reproduction and transformation of specific practices and for sometimes supportive, sometimes uneasy relations between them. It is common to think of practices as consumers, simply competing for resources, but the conclusion that understandings of space and time are usefully understood as *outcomes* of such relations complicates this analysis. It does so by suggesting that in competing and collaborating with each other, certain practices establish the terms and conditions on which others interact. Whatever their basis, relations between practices are important in shaping the availability, distribution and circulation of elements, in configuring loose bundles and dense complexes, and in consequently making some future linkages more likely than others. At the end of Chapter 4, 'Recruitment, defection and reproduction', we referred to Pred's discussion of dominant projects, these being sets of practices and around which individual and collective careers revolve. We are now in a position to think about how practices, and sets of practice, acquire dominant status. In the next section we consider two methods of approaching this problem.

SELECTION AND INTEGRATION

In innovation studies, the notion of dominant design has been used to explain how certain products and technological solutions define the terms on which others compete (and collaborate). Firms that succeed in establishing dominant designs out-do their rivals and in the same move, change the nature of the 'game' in which all are then involved. For writers like Tushman and Anderson (1986), the process of achieving technological dominance is generally one in which rivals are weeded out through competition, typically for investment, consumers or markets. In their words: 'technological experimentation and competition persists within a product class until a dominant design emerges as a synthesis of a number of proven concepts' (1986: 441). As with paradigms of scientific enquiry, dominant designs set the scene for further incremental development. And as with scientific knowledge, breaking through incumbent regimes and overturning dominant designs requires radical rather than incremental innovation (Abernathy and Clark, 1985).

The multi-level model of innovation introduced by Rip and Kemp (1998) and developed by Geels (2002, 2005; Geels and Schot, 2007, 2010) builds on these ideas. It suggests that new sociotechnical arrangements develop in niches; that innovations at this 'micro' level are shaped by and have consequences for the formation of 'meso'-level regimes and that these in turn structure and are structured by 'macro'-level landscapes. Since each level constitutes a selection environment for the one below, linkages are progressively denser and paths more dependent, meaning that landscapes are harder to change, and change more slowly than regimes or niches. In effect, dominant arrangements are those embedded at higher levels.

This scheme has been used to great effect in describing trajectories of sociotechnical change and in showing how incoming and incumbent systems intersect. For the most part, studies in this tradition focus on the careers of specific technologies (steam power, systems of hygiene, automobility etc.) and on related transitions in markets, technoscientific knowledge, cultural and symbolic meanings, infrastructures and user practices. This makes sense, especially when dominance is defined in terms of market share. There is no market for practices as such, but it is possible to represent changing patterns (e.g. of diet, food preservation and consumption) in similar terms.

The recent history of freezing illustrates this potential. In becoming a kind of dominant design, freezing and refrigeration have transformed the global food business and related systems of distribution, management and production, reconfiguring patterns of consumption along with a host of domestic practices including those of storing and preparing food (Garnett and Jackson, 2007).

In order to analyse this process in terms of a multi-level model of sociotechnical innovation we would need to consider the disappearance and cultivation of different forms of competence. This would not be difficult to do. When freezers were first introduced in the UK, many books were produced explaining what these appliances were for and how to use them to best effect (Ellis, 1969, 1976, 1978). As freezing took hold, previously important techniques like those of curing, pickling and preserving fell into decline and new 'user practices' emerged. Having traced these developments in detail we could then relate them to other meso-level innovations, for instance in the production of freezer-dependent ready foods, networks of frozen food distribution and kitchen design. An account of this kind would help show how freezing won out over its rivals, how it changed as it became embedded in society, and how its embedding has, in turn, changed the structure of food provisioning (Shove and Southerton, 2000).

Like other such narratives this is a tale in which there are winners and losers and in which the freezer's success is attributed to its capacity to edge competing systems out of the picture. There are, however, other ways of interpreting the past, and other methods of explaining why freezing has become such a normal, and such an apparently inevitable part of daily life.

Rather than overthrowing competing forms of food preservation, cooking and provisioning, freezing has arguably strengthened connections between them. Interviews with 40 households in the UK give a sense of how freezers figure in daily life (Hand and Shove, 2007: 83). This research, which deals with freezing-practices rather than the history of refrigerating technologies, indicated that freezing was vital for the reproduction of many very different routines. For example, some households valued freezers as instruments of planning, while others used them as a means of *avoiding* the need to think ahead. For some people, freezers were essential tools within a pattern of self-service catering and individual snacking; for others they were just as essential in maintaining routines and ideologies of home cooking and collective consumption.

The freezer's role has, in addition, evolved over time and as a consequence of related developments in systems of food provisioning and diet. For example, ideas about food have changed since the 1970s when freezers became items of mass consumption. In the intervening years, growing distrust of ready-prepared meals has reconfigured the meanings in circulation around the freezer and its contents. This is important in that the symbolic status of frozen food is relevant for the freezer's role in daily life. From this point of view, freezers act as a kind of relay device, condensing and materialising otherwise abstract concepts of care, health and convenience as these flow through associated practices of cooking, parenting and managing the home.

There is no denying the overall significance of freezing and refrigeration in the contemporary food system. But how has this position arisen and how is it sustained? One interpretation is that regimes of frozen food provisioning have developed at the expense of other rival possibilities. A second is that freezing has secured such a central position not by overriding existing arrangements but by becoming a co-dependent part of them.

Multi-level analyses of stability and change emphasize one-way tracks of path-dependence. These do not necessarily exclude parallel accounts of more fluid patterns of multi-sited anchoring. However, each approach draws attention to significantly different forms of positive and negative interconnection. The first highlights competitive relations and their impact on the selection environments of the future. The second suggests that webs of co-dependence are not evenly arranged, that they include nodes, knots, relays and points of convergence and amplification, and that the emergence of dominant systems and projects depends on how practices are linked, and not (only) on their capacity to compete. This underlines the importance of identifying and analysing types and com-binations of spatial and temporal links while remembering that these connections are living tissue: they do not exist ready-made, but are con-tinually re-woven as practices are reproduced (Ingold, 2008).

In the first part of this chapter we distinguished between loose bun-dles and denser, stickier complexes of practice, also describing arrange-ments in which patterns of sequential order and periodicity combine, and in which serendipity is common. It may be that configurations less constrained by path dependencies or by strict temporal order are better able to accommodate diversion and interruption. In these situations temporary defection, multi-tasking and contamination between prac-tices is perhaps more likely than when practices are held together by strong routines. Since everyday life consists of all these forms at once one might, in theory, seek to describe the overall texture of this emer-gent fabric and characterize the threads and ties of which it is made (this is a theme to which we return in Chapter 6, 'Circuits of reproduction'). Before moving on we bring this chapter to a close with a rather more tangible discussion of how links between practices are experienced, and what their coordination feels like on a daily basis.

COORDINATING DAILY LIFE

How do bundles, complexes and other such configurations of practice shape the organization of the day? On weekdays, most Europeans are awake at 7 a.m. and asleep again by 11 p.m. This remarkably regular pattern, an outcome of millions of fragments, moments and private episodes of synchronization, supports Lefebvre's claim that: 'In one day in the modern world, everybody does more or less the same things at more or less the same times, but each person is really alone in doing it' (Lefebvre, 2004: 75). Tidal movements of waking, sleeping and commuting, along with others that give rise to everyday experiences of routine and rhythm, arguably constitute the pulse of society. Many contend that this pulse is changing and that what goes on between and around the hours of 7 a.m. and 11 p.m. is becoming increasingly complicated, varied and unpredictable.

Analyses of why this might be so take different forms. Schor (1991) and Hochschild (2001) both focus on the relation between time devoted to paid employment and the quantity and quality of the free time that remains. Others suggest that experiences of being rushed and pressed for time relate to the fact that collective societal rhythms based on the seasons or on the institutional ordering of the week and the weekend, the evening and the day have lost the grip they once had. Now that shops are open all hours and that mobile communication technologies mean that arrangements to meet can be made and broken at a moment's notice, individuals have to negotiate their own ways through timescapes simultaneously characterized by fragmentation, such that days consist of many small episodes, and expansion through multi-tasking. According to research for Yahoo, multi-tasking allows people to pack the equivalent of 43 hours into the day (Hess, 2006). The implication here is that experiences of rush are not, or not simply due to a lack of time, but to the fact that time has become harder to organize and manage.

In concentrating on time, these accounts miss the point that experiences and episodes are embedded in, and are outcomes of, changing relations between practices. In other words, there is not so much a squeeze of time (Southerton, 2003) as a squeeze of practice-related injunctions of sequencing, coordination and personalized scheduling. As Southerton reminds us, 'practices come with sets of requirements necessary for competent and meaningful engagement' (2006: 440), many of which have consequences for the time required and for how this should be organized and scheduled.

Although people often think of time pressure as a personal affliction and as a sign of their own failure to keep on top of things and retain control (Thompson, 1996), the problem almost certainly lies with the sets of practices they are carrying and with the demands these make in terms of duration, timing and sequence. Is it that practices are, overall, becoming more demanding and hungrier for time? Have the time-profiles of specific social practices changed in ways that generate rush and fragmentation? Given the special challenges of synchronization and coordination, are more solitary practices edging collective ones out of the frame, or vice versa? Similarly, is the effort entailed in coordinating people, things and places increasing, perhaps due to the character of social and material networks (Larsen et al., 2006)?

When framed like this, understanding the spatial and temporal rhythm of society is in essence a matter of understanding how some practices flourish and others fade; how qualities of frequency, duration and sequence emerge; how practices integrate to form bundles and complexes; and how such configurations resonate, amplify or destroy each other. In short, the pace and rhythm of social life can be understood as an outcome, at any one moment, of the totality of current life paths and associated projects and practices. What Lefebvre refers to as 'the rhythm of society' is arguably no more but also no less than the cumulative and co-existing interaction of this totality. Accordingly, trends in the temporal and spatial character of daily life are symptomatic of underlying transformations in relations between practices and in the way they weave together. In the next chapter we examine processes involved in maintaining, sustaining and transforming these textures, patterns and relationships.

CIRCUITS OF REPRODUCTION

6

In Chapter 5 we wrote about how practices connect. We discussed forms of competition and collaboration and identified stronger, weaker and more and less extensive connections across space and time. We went on to suggest that daily rhythms and dominant projects reflect and reproduce such links. In this chapter we investigate the forms of feedback that connect successive performances in ways that enable mutual adjustment between practices.

It is obvious that past performances create and limit opportunities for future development. There is also no doubt that existing practices have multiple consequences, making 'courses of action easier, harder, simpler, more complicated, shorter, longer, ill-advised, promising of gain, disruptive, facilitating, obligatory or proscribed, acceptable or unacceptable, more or less relevant, riskier or safer, more or less feasible, more or less likely to induce ridicule or approbation' (Schatzki, 2002: 226). But how are these features folded into any one moment of performance, or into the trajectories of practices as they develop over time?

Giddens uses the concept of a 'reproduction circuit' to address this problem and to show how the reflexive monitoring of action relates, through the duality of structure, to what he terms 'structural properties' and 'structural principles' (Giddens, 1984: 191). In his rather schematic account, circuits of reproduction include loops of feedback (and feed forward) between individual actors engaged in monitoring the continuous flow of activity, and between these and the structural properties of social systems. Although described as circuits of 'reproduction', such relationships do not ensure continuity. As Giddens explains, 'Analysing circuits of reproduction, it should be clear, is not equivalent to identifying the sources of stability alone. They serve indeed to indicate some of the main forms of change involved in the transition from one type of societal totality to another' (Giddens, 1984: 191). The idea that practices and sets of practices are sustained and transformed in this way makes a lot of sense, but can we pin the circuitry down, and if so, what does it look like in daily life?

In approaching this task we build on ideas introduced in Chapter 4, 'Recruitment, defection and reproduction'. In that chapter we wrote about people as variously faithful carriers of practice. We talked then about how individuals are recruited, how practitioner-careers develop and what these trajectories mean, overall, for the fate and future of the practices involved. We now home-in on the enactment of linkage: How does one performance of a practice relate to the next? What kind of monitoring and feedback occur? Equally important, what are the forms of 'cross-referencing and interdependent know-hows' (Schatzki et al., 2001: 50) through which practices shape each other. Having considered a number of possibilities, we end with a more general discussion of the proposition that circuits of reproduction themselves evolve with potentially significant consequences for the texture and rhythm of daily life and for how such patterns are formed (Knorr Cetina, 2005b).

We begin by distinguishing between forms of monitoring, which matter for the *development of practices over time*, and types of cross-referencing, relevant for *relations between co-existing practices*. We discuss both with reference to the enactment of practices-as-performances and in relation to the careers of practices-as-entities (see Chapter 1). This gives us four situations to consider:

- monitoring practices-as-performances
- monitoring practices-as-entities
- cross-referencing practices-as-performances
- cross-referencing practices-as-entities.

In the next four sections we work with this scheme, using it to identify and illustrate different types of circuitry and show how these combine. We start with instances in which moments of performance are connected, over time, by basic forms of recording, measurement and reaction.

MONITORING PRACTICES-AS-PERFORMANCES

Monitoring, whether instant or delayed, provides practitioners with feedback on the outcomes and qualities of past performance. To the extent that this feeds forward into what they do next it is significant for the persistence, transformation and decay of the practices concerned. This takes multiple forms.

In many cases it is difficult to separate monitoring from doing. Making a batch of cement mortar requires constant observation and adaptation: adding a bit more liquid, mixing, checking and adding again until the consistency is just right. In this case the human body, and especially the senses of sight, smell and touch, feature as primary instruments both of monitoring and of responsive adaptation (Dant, 2010). However, this is not the only kind of feedback involved. The embodied and/or codified memory of previous mixes also provides a template against which the present batch is evaluated. Indeed, it is only because knowledge is carried forward in this way that it is possible to tell when the consistency is 'right'. Further layers of judgement come into play if the cement is mixed by a trainee bricklayer. In this case the apprentice's performance may be evaluated days later by an outside observer. Not only is the gap between doing and feedback then greater, it is, in addition, mediated by a range of formalized instruments (score sheets, written criteria etc.). In situations like these the consequences of performance monitoring matter for what happens next across a range of possible scales – did the mix turn out well, does the apprentice pass the test and move on to the next grade?

At whatever level we focus, this example suggests that self-monitoring or monitoring by others is part of, and not somehow outside, the enactment of a practice. Determining what it means to do well or to do a practice at all (what are the minimum conditions of the practice?) is, in a sense, integral to the performance. Amongst other things this means that the instruments of recording (the body, the score sheet, the trainee's CV) have a constitutive and not an innocent role. The recent history of heart rate monitoring is interesting in this regard. As described below, heart rate monitoring has become part of and has in the same move modified the meaning and experience of physical exercise for millions of people.

Until a few years ago heart rate monitoring only took place in hospitals and surgeries. Though useful as a trace of physical condition, and sometimes significant in diagnosing trouble, monitoring was important as input to and periodic feedback on programmes of treatment and care. Today, portable heart rate monitors are used around the world, not for medical reasons but as an increasingly integrated part of an expanding range of sporting activities. In these new settings, heart rate monitors reveal and quantify changes in previously unmeasured but not entirely unknown aspects of bodily performance. Polar Electro's slogan, 'Listen to your body', emphasizes the value of constant recording for a proper understanding of physical condition, target-setting and motivation. Equipped with a fitness monitor, an individual body becomes a different kind of knowable, calculable and administrative object. In this role, the body generates data, comparative analysis of which influences the demands and fitness regimes to which the body is then subjected.

Some argue that forms of self-governance and discipline like those enabled by heart rate monitors and a plethora of other auditing instruments are symptomatic of a more diffuse transformation in how social order is reproduced (Miller and Rose, 2008). Discussions of this kind generally focus on the relation between self-governing practitioners, the distributed power structures of society and the means by which these structures are unwittingly enacted and sustained. This is an important topic, but as we are about to see, similar processes underpin the evolution of practices-as-entities and hence the range of pursuits in which social actors are actually and potentially engaged.

MONITORING PRACTICES-AS-ENTITIES

In Chapter 4, 'Recruitment, defection and reproduction', we argued that the changing contours of practices-as-entities are shaped by the sum total of what practitioners do, by the variously faithful ways in which performances are enacted over time and by the scale and commitment of the cohorts involved. We also noticed that practices-as-entities develop as streams of consistently faithful and innovative performances intersect. This makes sense, but how are the transformative effects of such encounters played out? More specifically, how are definitions and understandings of what it is to *do* a practice mediated and shared, and how do such representations change over time?

The relatively well-documented, relatively recent career of snow-boarding provides some clues as to what might be involved. This is a good case to look at on a number of counts. First, the history appears to be one in which a user-driven innovation, born of a combination of surfing and skiing, has been institutionalized. Second, these develop-ments seem to have come about through contest and fission within the community of practitioners. As a result there are now different ways of doing snowboarding. Third, current variants attract different kinds of recruits and are in turn animated and sustained in distinctive but not entirely unrelated ways.

Most commentators agree that the character of snowboarding has been shaped by an ongoing and not always harmonious relation with skiing (Humphreys, 2003). In the early days, snowboarding was defined by an initially rebellious image cultivated by youthful pioneers who did battle with the 'stuffy' institutions that controlled the ski-slopes. The snow-boarding sub-culture, associated with an ethos of freedom, self-expression and artistic style, proved to be hugely attractive: new recruits flooded in. As the number of snowboarders rose, established commercial interests latched on to the opportunities this presented for product development and profit. This helped establish snowboarding as a legitimate sport, while widening rifts within it. By the time the Fédération Internationale du Ski (representing the establishment) included snowboarding in the 1998 Winter Olympic Games in Japan, the split was clear. As one experienced snowboarder put it, 'It's almost like there's going to be a different sport – freeriding is one thing, and training and competing and now going to the Olympics is going to be another' (Humphreys, 2003: 422).

If we take a step back, we can see that splitting, merging and recombining are normal processes. Snowboarding techniques developed as skills established in windsurfing and skateboarding migrated from one field to another. Some of these 'new' styles and tricks were absorbed without trouble, but others led to splits and fractures in the practice as a whole. When this happens, new variants emerge. Developments of this kind are relevant for who is drawn into the sport: Is snowboarding something for aspiring athletes? Is it about doing tricks just for fun? Patterns of recruitment and defection are crucial, but if we are to understand what snowboarding 'is' at any one moment, and if we are to figure out how the image and the substance of the sport evolves, we need to identify the means by which different versions of the practice-as-entity relate to each other over time. Methods of naming and recording constitute one form of connective tissue.

In *naming* tricks like the ollie, the nollie, the rippey flip and the chicken salad, snowboarders recognize and temporarily stabilize specific moves. Such descriptions map onto templates of performance – to an idea of what it is to do an ollie, and what it means to do one well. In the world of Olympic competition, conventions are formalized and described with greater precision. Judges are, for example, expected to give credit for height above the halfpipe rim, for higher risk-taking and for sequences such as back-to-back 900-degree spins (2 ½ revolutions) done in opposite directions (Ruibal, 2006). Needless to say, these criteria are themselves controversial. Not all agree that they capture what the sport is 'really' about. These controversies in turn demonstrate the importance of rules and descriptions: in valuing certain skills and qualities above others, they define the present state of play and the direction in which techniques and technologies evolve.

Technologies are themselves important in stabilizing and transforming the contours of a practice. In producing snowboards of different length, weight, width and form, the industry caters to – and in a sense produces – the increasingly diverse needs of different types of user. Specialized boards are now available. Some are good for certain snow conditions, for half-pipe performance, or for speed or style (Thorpe, 2005: 79). Developments of this kind contribute to the ongoing setting and re-setting of conventions and standards. In addition, and in so far as they script user performance, these designs have a bearing on the skills involved. On both counts, the materiality of the snowboard is not 'just' an element in the practice: it is also crucial in facilitating some but not other techniques and in inspiring some but not other kinds of innovation.

Describing and materializing represent two modes of monitoring in the sense that they capture and to some extent formalize aspects of performance in terms of which subsequent enactments are defined and differentiated. A third mode lies in processes of mediation which also constitute channels of circulation. Within some snowboarding subcultures, making and sharing videos has become part of the experience. These films, along with magazines, websites and exhibitions, provide tangible records of individual performance and collectively reflect changing meanings of the sport within and between its various forms. Put simply, they allow actual and potential practitioners to 'keep up' with what is happening at the practice's leading edge(s).

The relative significance of these modes – description, materialization and mediation – may change as practices stabilize or fragment. In addition, there may be systematic differences in exactly how formal rule-governed variants and more anarchic styles of snowboarding are reproduced. We have picked on snowboarding not because its career is typical, or because the processes involved are of enormous significance. Having described some of the routes through which it has developed, we are nonetheless in a position to see that standards, in the form of rules, descriptions, materials and representations, constitute templates and benchmarks in terms of which present performances are evaluated and in relation to which future variants develop.

To this we add one further point. The different means by which the practice is known and carried combine in ways that have emergent consequences of their own. In snowboarding, competitions and events are key sites in which resources of legitimacy, money and reputation accumulate and disappear, and in which social capital is exchanged and translated. Such processes are reminiscent of what Latour and Woolgar refer to as 'cycles of credibility' (1986). Their study of laboratory life showed how the currencies of scientific research – citations, reputation, research funding – fuelled each other. In the situations they describe, research funding led to research papers that enhanced reputations in ways which made it easier to get more research funding and so on. Similar forms of positive feedback no doubt apply in other quite unrelated fields, doing so in ways that engender, consolidate and destroy communities of practice.

It has been useful to distinguish between the forms of monitoring and feedback that link one instance of performance to the next, and those implicated in the unfolding careers of practices-as-entities. But it is important to remember that they connect. We comment briefly on three ways in which this occurs. The first has to do with how the careers of individuals and practices intersect. At a very basic level, it is good to know you are doing well. Even the most casual forms of monitoring reveal (and in a sense constitute) levels of performance. In this role, signs of progress are often important in encouraging further effort and investment of time and energy (Sudnow, 1993). The details of how performances are evaluated (when, how often, by whom) consequently structure the careers of individual practitioners *and* the career path that the practice itself affords. This internal structure is itself of relevance for the number of practitioners involved and the extent of their commitment (see the discussion of Lave and Wenger, 1991 in Chapter 4).

Second, methods of measurement, like heart rate monitors and stock-market tickers, may end up changing the performances *and* the practices they are designed to monitor. Something of this sort happens when people construct exercise regimes around target heart rates. But there are many other more extensive examples. Alex Preda's fascinating account of the framing of finance is one. He describes how the stock-market ticker reconfigured the rhythm of users' responses, the timing of actions and reactions and the structure of financial activity itself. As he explains, the ticker came to bind 'investors and brokers to its ticks', demanding their 'constant presence, attention and observation' (Preda, 2009: 132) and engendering feelings and emotions not always consistent with the rational pursuit of profit. In this rather complicated case, technologies of feedback transformed the elements of financial practice and the performances involved.

Finally, systems of classification and standards constitute what Bowker and Star refer to as 'invisible mediators of action' (2000b). They do so by establishing templates in terms of which performances are compared; by defining what any one enactment is a performance *of* (this being in part determined by how performance is recorded); and by reconfiguring elements of the practice and the manner in which they are integrated.

These examples of monitoring, recording, calibrating and feedback give a sense of the means by which performances and practices constitute each other and how moments of enactment are linked over time. Our next task is to show how co-existing practices shape each other in the moment of performance and over the longer run.

CROSS-REFERENCING PRACTICES-AS-PERFORMANCES

In so far as time spent on one practice is not available to another, performances are exclusive. From this point of view the enactment of one practice is of consequence for others in that it simply prevents them from taking place (Pred, 1981). Not all cross-practice relations are as crude as this and there are other more subtle ways in which practices-as-performances condition each other. As we noticed in the previous chapter, sequencing and synchronization are both important for the scheduling of daily life and for how practices come together in space and time. We now turn to the question of *how* these connections are enacted and reproduced.

Southerton's study of domestic time management gives a general sense of what the conduct of one practice means for another (2003). His research indicates that some households deliberately rush parts of the day in order to create unhurried periods of 'quality' time elsewhere in their schedule. In effect, short-cuts and compromises in the performance of certain practices are accepted because they allow for the 'proper' enactment of others. Cross-practice trade-offs like these play out over different periods of time: many take place in the frame of a day, but some are conceptualized in terms of years, decades or lifetimes. Understanding these sorts of arrangements helps in understanding how patchworks of practice are stitched together and how people organize their lives (or how their lives are organized by the practices they carry).

Issues of sequencing and real-time management are important in daily life, but how are these arrangements reproduced and what forms of feedback are involved? Having established that practices are squeezed and stretched in relation to each other (Southerton, 2003), and that personal and collective schedules are outcomes of complex and emergent processes, we need to zoom in a bit closer. When we do so, we catch sight of some of the mediating devices involved in managing these relations. We comment briefly on instruments used in sequencing and synchronizing, starting with clocks.

In many households, morning routines depend on precise and accurate timing. The minutes between getting up and leaving home are filled by a sequence of practices, each of which can take only so long. Any deviation, dallying over breakfast or getting up late, throws the schedule out of kilter. For those locked into an established pattern there is often no need to check the clock, but when routines are disturbed it is important to keep an eye on the time.

The widespread use of clocks and watches together with shared conventions about how time should be described and known constitutes a coordinative infrastructure that is arguably essential for the conduct of modern life. For Simmel, 'the technique of metropolitan life is unimaginable without the most punctual integration of all activities and mutual relations into a stable and impersonal time schedule' (2002: 125). Zerubavel's historical review of the standardization of time emphasizes the significance of coordination. As he explains, 'the need to standardize temporal reference so as to allow for a coordination of behavior exists even at the lowest level of social organization. Yet the complexity of the problem is directly proportional to the size of the social system involved' (1982: 4). Effective and reliable postal systems and functioning railway networks brought communities together. But before these links could be made, those same communities had to subscribe to standardized systems of reckoning time. Clock time remains essential, but its status as *the* common currency of coordinating and scheduling appears to be changing.

In Urry's view, the clock-time of pocket/wrist watches has recently been 'supplemented by a negotiated "network" or fluid time of mobile communication' (2007: 173). Studies of mobile phone use generally focus on the rate at which this technology has diffused, or the impact it has had on conventions of conversation (Laurier, 2001). However, some commentators are interested in the ways in which mobile messaging (texting, phoning, mobile emailing) influences synchronous cross-referencing between practices.

Ling and Yttri write about how mobile phones permit 'the arrangement and rearrangement of basic logistical details on the fly' (2002: 144). This potential is an important aspect of what these authors refer to as 'micro-coordination'. Ito and Okabe (2005) explain how this works out for Japanese youngsters wanting to meet with friends in central Tokyo. Rather than spending hours waiting

> at landmarks such as Hachiko Square in Shibuya or Roppongi crossing, making occasional forays to a payphone to check for messages at home or at a friend's home, [teens and twenty-somethings] agree on a general time and place (Shibuya, Saturday late afternoon), and exchange approximately 5 to 15 messages that progressively narrow in on a precise time and place, two or more points eventually converging in a coordinated dance through the urban jungle. As the meeting time nears, contact via messaging and voice becomes more concentrated, eventually culminating in face-to-face contact.
>
> (Ito and Okabe, 2005: 267)

This is not a strategy confined to the young. As Urry recognizes, there are many situations in which coordination, previously 'finalized before departure', is now 'negotiated and performed on the move' (2007: 173).

Ling and Yttri argue that mobile micro-coordination results in what they refer to as a 'softening of time, associated with the fact that it is now possible to call and let people know that one is late' (2002: 143). But is this of further significance for the ways in which practices shape each other? For example, does the possibility of instant adjustment increase the range of practices in which many people are involved? Does real-time coordination generate more or less leeway in the timing and sequencing of what people do? Are patterns of inattention and disengagement changing as practices are dropped or cut short in response to news that something else is going on? Equally, are novel practices developing as a result? In thinking about these questions it is important to consider how technologies of 'micro'-coordination relate to those that operate on a global scale.

In the previous chapter we noticed how practices bundle together in spaces like the office and the home. As we saw then, physical proximity was often relevant for (and sometimes a consequence of) sequence and synchronization. It is now clear that virtual connections can be just as important. The telegraph, the telephone and more recent arrivals like email, Facebook and Skype have facilitated variously extensive, and variously intensive forms of interaction at a distance. In bringing more points of reference into play, and in now doing so all at once rather than a bit at a time, these technologies make a qualitative difference to the ways in which practices connect.

The consequences are unclear, and are in any case sure to vary, but it seems reasonable to suggest that modes of cross-referencing characterized by many little prompts, each modulating sequences of practices and their (co)location are likely to have ongoing and emergent effects for the performance of individual practices and for relations between them. From this point of view, mobile communication, like the emergence of the 24-hour society or clock-time itself, have an active and potentially transformative role in promoting, and in some cases preventing, the reproduction of relations between practices.

We have surely not provided a comprehensive account of how the enactment of one practice shapes another, but in detailing modes and methods of sequencing and synchronization we have shown that moments of performance reproduce and reflect qualities of spacing and timing, some proximate, some remote. It is in this sense that individual practices 'make' the environments that others inhabit. We have also shown that although these recursive relations are constituted through forms of feedback, these are not of the sort involved in calibrating performances against a template of effective accomplishment, or of the kind that feeds forward into future innovation.

CROSS-REFERENCING PRACTICES-AS-ENTITIES

As represented in Chapter 5, bundles of practice are more loosely connected than complexes which are held together by stronger, thicker bonds of co-dependence. In trying to characterize the 'circuits of reproduction' that keep these arrangements in place, and keep them in motion, we begin by borrowing Knorr Cetina's concept of epistemic objects.

Karin Knorr Cetina (1997) introduced the notion of an 'epistemic object' to help make sense of the everyday power of necessarily incomplete lines of scientific enquiry and to help understand their capacity to enthuse individuals and attract and organize diverse sets of resources and practices. In a later article, Knorr Cetina and Bruegger (2000) explore the relevance of treating 'the market' in similar terms; in developing these ideas they suggest the market has 'an independent existence as a "lifeform"' presenting new challenges to traders who simultaneously create this 'object' to which they are in thrall. As described here, the market is an unpredictable, uncontrollable yet demanding entity, always requiring sometimes subtle and sometimes radical re-arrangements of co-requisite sets or bundles of practice. Zwick and Dholakia's (2006) analysis of online trading and personal investing suggests that ordinary consumers and professional traders confront and reproduce 'the market' in much the same way. In theory, brands (Lury, 2004), policy problems (Miettinen and Virkkunen, 2005; Voβ et al., 2006), lifestyle unities (McCracken, 1988) and sub-cultures (Cohen, 1987) have comparable status. Like other objects of knowledge, they are 'always in the process of being materially defined, they continually acquire new properties and change the ones they have' (Knorr Cetina and Bruegger, 2000: 149).

Although both have a filtering effect, framing, enabling and constraining some but not other trajectories, this continually transformative aspect sets epistemic objects apart from Kuhnian paradigms (Kuhn,

1970). It also serves to distinguish them from the top-down designs of powerful actors seeking to bring selected practices together in spatial and temporal bundles and complexes, or to force them apart. When epistemic objects are involved, relevant processes of fracture and re-mapping go on through and as a consequence of referencing, cross-referencing, and referencing again. In this analysis, epistemic objects have a dual role: featuring as outcomes of inter-practice relations and as entities around which iterative, recurrent and largely uncontrollable but not entirely arbitrary cycles of framing, spilling over, divergence, adaptation and change (D'Adderio, 2008: 770) are ordered.

Knorr Cetina's analysis provides us with a way of thinking about how links between practices are reproduced. It underscores both the provisional character of these connections and their power to act back. But again, there is more to say about how these reproductive circuits operate. In what follows we focus first on methods of aggregation and then on the coordinative role of elements (material, meaning, competence). These are not the only forms of cross-referencing involved, but in describing them we illustrate some of the routes through which practices-as-entities are brought together in space and time.

Aggregation

Many objects of public concern are made visible, and in a sense simply made, through processes of statistical aggregation. These processes sustain meso-level discourses and categories that have orchestrating and coordinative effects in their own right, and that integrate otherwise unrelated practices. As we are about to see, objects of concern, like obesity, are simultaneously reproduced in 'micro' and 'macro' forms as data recorded on such humble instruments as bathroom scales are added, analysed and aggregated to produce a problem of epic proportion.

Bathroom scales and tape measures are often important for those who want to gain or lose weight. Much like the heart rate monitors discussed earlier, these devices permit forms of monitoring that influence cooking, eating, shopping and exercising and bring these disparate practices together as part of a common project, namely that of shedding or gaining kilos. By stepping back on the scales – a day, a week or six months

later – individuals are able to track their progress. For them, the numbers on the display provide a form of feedback, prompting further revision (or not) of eating and exercise regimes.

However, weight is of more than individual interest. Measurements
based on thousands of readings around the world reveal the changing
weight of nations. When aggregated and organized with the help of
standardized tools of interpretation like the Body Mass Index, 'calculated as weight (kg) divided by height squared (m^2)', these data can be
'used to classify underweight, overweight and obesity in adults' (Branca
et al., 2007: 2). The trends are striking. According to the World Health
Organization, 'Excess body weight poses one of the most serious public
health challenges of the 21st century' (Branca et al., 2007: 1). In the
USA and in the World Health Organization's European Region the
prevalence of obesity has tripled in the last two decades.

These figures have inspired a raft of initiatives designed to modify
national diets and increase levels of sport and exercise (DCMS/Strategy
Unit, 2002). In the realm of public policy, official documents emphasize
the need to mobilize and promote anti-obesity strategies across different
tiers and departments of government (House of Commons Health
Committee, 2004: 2). As with personal dieting regimes, these efforts are
themselves subject to recurrent evaluation and revision. In England
regular health surveys, the equivalent of the national bathroom scales,
are essential instruments of monitoring and feedback across a range of
policy domains.

In short, representing obesity as a problem of public health involves
two interdependent moves: first, the aggregation of individual readings;
and second, the production of a discursive space in which otherwise
disconnected practices (eating, exercise) are drawn together. Now that
obesity is established as an epidemic and now that it is subject to concerted treatment, the problem is certain to change shape, not because
citizens will necessarily heed government advice or step more lightly on
their bathroom scales, but because this coordinative discourse, sustained
and transformed by a repertoire of associated instruments of intervention and monitoring, has a life of its own. As Evans explains, the concept of obesity brings multiple practices together within its moralizing
fold (2006: 261).

In due course, aggregate representations and policy discourses feed back into the bathroom itself – people come to read their own bodies in a correspondingly moral way (Evans, 2006: 261). According to Boero, widespread use of the Body Mass Index (BMI) has had an impact on how people think about themselves. In her words, it is no longer enough to check in the mirror or glance at the scales: 'to more accurately assess the risk we also need to know, as individuals, our BMI, our body fat ratio, and the precise distribution of fat on our bodies to be sure that we aren't obese or at risk of obesity' (2007: 52).

This brief discussion of obesity illustrates some of the ways in which discourses and technologies of measurement and monitoring constitute 'epistemic objects' in terms of which practices are conjoined and associated, one to another. In emphasizing related processes of recording, observation and state analysis, this account has much in common with Donzelot's analysis of the making and policing of specific models of the 'family' (Donzelot and Hurley, 1980), with Knorr Cetina's own work on 'the flow architecture of financial markets' (Knorr Cetina, 2003), and with histories of hygiene as a concept through which bodies, surfaces, germs and practices of laundering and bathing have been brought together in new relation. This is rarely a matter of discursive categorization alone. In the case of hygiene, as with obesity, the formation and reproduction of coordinative epistemic objects depends on specific conjunctions of what we have described as the elements of practice. If we home in even closer, it is possible to detect the changing constellations of materials, meanings and forms of competence on which these circuits depend.

Elements of coordination

In Chapter 3 we wrote about how elements of meaning, materiality and competence travel and we described some of the forms of transportation, codification and classification involved. At that point we were primarily interested in elements as ingredients of practice, hence our focus on circulation, distribution and access. We now come back to elements, this time viewing them as instruments of coordination. In their role as aggregators, accumulators, relays and vehicles, elements are more than necessary building blocks: they are also relevant for the manner in which practices relate to each other and for how these relations change over time.

There are various ways in which this works. Where elements figure in several practices at once they constitute a kind of common ground. For example, when the meaning of being fat becomes part of practices like those of shopping, exercising and eating, it becomes a point of *connection* between them. We referred to similar situations in Chapter 2, where we considered the relation between driving and repairing cars, and concepts of masculinity. In cases of this kind, elemental links are not fixed like rods or wires, but are better understood as zones of overlap and intersection.

Other metaphors are required to show how certain elements facilitate the aggregation of others. Debates within science and technology studies shed some light on what is involved. According to Latour, objects which have the properties of being 'mobile but also immutable, presentable, readable and combinable with one another' (1990: 6) are essential for coordinating and mustering resources and permitting action at a distance. Writing (and reading) is one simple example, hence the conclusion that 'inscription, and in particular its printed reproduction, makes possible the concentration of a far wider range of allies than had previously been possible' (Law, 1986: 255). John Law explores similar themes in an article on sixteenth-century Portuguese navigation in which he explains how a distinctive combination of human and non-human actors (ships, astrolabes and disciplined sailors) came together to constitute a sociotechnical complex capable of exerting enormous influence around the world. Law makes much of the necessary stability of this hybrid machine, the effective functioning of which depended on the faithful reproduction of 'a structure of heterogeneous elements containing envoys which are mobile, durable, forceful and able to return' (1986: 257). In his analysis, certain conjunctions of elements (materials, meanings, competences) permitted the coordination and spectacular aggregation of others.

Elements may not be quite as immutable as Law suggests. As we saw in Chapter 3, 'The life of elements', mobility and circulation often involves some kind of transformation. Even so, it is perfectly possible

that materials, along with meanings and abstracted forms of competence, are 'superimposed, reshuffled, recombined, and summarized'
with the result that totally new phenomena emerge (Latour, 1990) *and*
that new relations between practices are forged.

In thinking about how elements figure in the more extensive circuits
of reproduction involved in sustaining (and changing) relations between
practices, we need to remember that elements are in many important
respects formed and transformed through their integration both in individual practices and in different sets of practices at once. Going full
circle, relations between practices are themselves important for the elements of which individual practices are made. To complicate matters
further, the ways in which practices develop over time is clearly significant for how bundles and complexes of practice intersect at any one
moment. In the last part of this chapter we take stock of the different
circuits of reproduction discussed this far and explore the possibility
that the manner in which elements, practices and relations between
them hang together are themselves subject to change.

INTERSECTING CIRCUITS

In this chapter we have built on the idea that if practices are to endure,
the elements of which they are made need to be linked together consistently and recurrently over time (circuit 1). How this works out is, in
turn, limited and shaped by the intended and unintended consequences
of previous and coexisting configurations (circuit 2). Our third step has
been to suggest that persistence and change depend upon feedback
between one instance or moment of enactment and another, and on patterns of mutual influence between co-existing practices (circuit 3). It is
through these three intersecting circuits that practices-as-entities come
into being and through these that they are transformed.

We have used a number of examples to show how such circuits operate in daily life. As we have seen, monitoring, broadly defined, has the
dual effect of spanning between past, present and future and of capturing individual performances in forms that can be aggregated to establish
the 'performance' of society as a whole. In their first role, tools of

comparison and evaluation provide users with feedback (some instant, some delayed) on the outcomes and consequences of past performance. This is significant for what they do next. Statistics – derived from local instances of measurement – have a similar role at an institutional level: revealing the impacts of policies past and steering strategies for the future.

In both settings, instruments of monitoring and cross-referencing are of some significance for exactly what does and does not fall into the realm of everyday calculability. For example, the recent introduction of portable heart rate monitors has transformed the relation between sports enthusiasts and their bodies. They do not just know they got, or are getting, a bit puffed, they can now see exactly when the heart rate rises, and by exactly how much. If they have a fancy device, they can download this data and store it for further reference. To the extent that such arrangements permit forms of feedback (either over time or between practices), they figure in one or more of the three circuits outlined above. This suggests that forms of recording and cross-referencing play an important part in the reproduction of practices *and* of relations between them. This is not an innocent role. As we have seen, devices like clocks and stock-market tickers do not merely provide data that are fed into some existing circuit. These and many other such arrangements transform the detailed operation of one or more circuits of reproduction, and in so doing structure both the reproduction of society and the means by which this takes place.

The idea that there might be societal trends in the ordering and organization of feedback (monitoring and cross-referencing) is not especially new, but it is hugely important for the dynamics of social practice. It is also important for those interested in modes of governance and organization. In *Political Anatomy of the Body*, David Armstrong (1983) shows how the socio-medical survey relocated the meaning and the practice of illness. As with some of the examples discussed above, it did so by aggregating, categorizing, normalizing and positioning cases (patients) one in relation to another. The key point here is that surveys and related methods of analysis changed the operation as well as the distribution of power. In Armstrong's words, entirely new conditions of possibility emerged as webs 'of investigation, observation and recording' were woven 'around individual bodies, their relationships and their subjectivity, in the name of health' (1983: 112).

Other writers document comparable processes of inscription through which '"objects" such as the economy, the enterprise, the social field and the family are rendered in a particular conceptual form and made amenable to intervention and regulation' (Miller and Rose, 2008: 30). The ordering and management of knowledge is central to this enterprise and to the means by which diverse domains of governmentality are established. As Armstrong explains, methods of aggregation and concentration are of consequence for spatial order and organization (Armstrong, 1995). Survey instruments underpinned and in a sense demanded new forms of surveillance medicine organized around the project of knowing and managing the health of the population as a whole. In this way, illness moved from the bedside and hospital out into the wider world.

Theories of governance tend to take the nation-state as their point of reference; and it is true, this is an important site of recording, analysing and intervention. However, it is increasingly easy to calibrate performances with reference to data gathered from around the world. This possibility has created conditions in which what Boero (2007) describes as 'epidemics of signification' are quick to take hold. Unlike traditional epidemics, these post-modern forms spread rapidly through the media, fuelled by the potential to benchmark and compare, and amplified by processes akin to those involved in the making of moral panics (Cohen, 1987). Obesity is one such case.

Many commentators refer to the speeding-up of society, and to the emergence of new forms of global interconnection (Urry, 2007) but Knorr Cetina goes further in arguing that there have been qualitative changes in the fabric of the social structure and threads and ties of which it is made. She writes about the development of 'global microstructures' characterized by 'forms of connectivity and coordination that combine global reach with microstructural mechanisms that instantiate self-organizing principles and patterns' (2005a: 214). These intriguing forms, which exist alongside, but outside more conventional structures, have distinctive capacities for change precisely because of the character of the connections of which they are composed. Compared to other modes of organization, they thrive in situations in which 'markets are too fast, and change too quickly to be "contained" by institutional orders. Global systems based on microstructural principles do not exhibit institutional complexity but rather the asymmetries, unpredictabilities and playfulness of complex (and dispersed) interaction patterns' (2005a: 214). In these situations, the circuits through which practices travel, mutate and reproduce exist beyond and outside what we normally recognize as social orders and systems. This is not simply a matter of saying that different people are involved. The point is that the nature of the connections, along with the terms of cross-referencing and monitoring, are themselves of a different order. Global microstructures consequently generate and are carried by 'scopic' modes of feedback characterized by a system 'of observation and projection that assembles on one surface dispersed and diverse activities, interpretations and representations which in turn orient and constrain the response of an audience' (Knorr Cetina and Preda, 2007: 126).

The emergence of such modes may be symptomatic of a more pervasive transformation in the circuitry of society itself. Whether or not this is so, it is clear that technologies and instruments of feedback, broadly defined, are of direct relevance in configuring circuits of reproduction that are, in turn, of equally direct consequence for the survival and transformation of relations between practices and the elements of which they are composed. It is also evident that seemingly neutral circuits of reproduction are skewed and slanted by patterns of inequality, these being patterns that are in turn perpetuated through the dominance and marginalization of specific practices and practice complexes.

With this observation we bring our analysis of the dynamics of social practice to a close. In the next chapter we take stock of the argument built and the contribution we have made to the analysis of stability and change. In the final chapter we consider the relevance of our approach for public policy: What might practice-oriented policy look like, and what new challenges and opportunities might it generate?

7

REPRESENTING THE DYNAMICS OF SOCIAL PRACTICE

At the start of this book we set ourselves the challenge of conceptualizing social order, stability and change and of doing so in a manner that was consistently and systematically informed by theories of practice. In this chapter we take stock of what we have achieved. We start by summarizing and reviewing the key features of our approach before considering its implications for the study of time and space. Our slimline interpretation of practice theory also helps in understanding how the circuits through which practices are reproduced sustain ways of life that are in different respects unequal and unsustainable. We do not go deep into the questions of power but we go far enough to set the scene for Chapter 8, a chapter in which we explore the prospect of deliberately promoting transitions in practice.

The bare bones of our account can be put in just a few sparse sentences. Practices-as-performances involve the active integration of elements (materials, meanings, competences). Practices-as-entities are constituted through such integrations (Chapter 2). Practices change when new elements are introduced or when existing elements are combined in new ways. Elements of meaning, materiality and competence are themselves outcomes of practice. Although they are generated and changed through moments of enactment, elements – being part of several practices at once – have somewhat independent lives of their own (Chapter 3). If practices are to survive they need to capture and retain practitioners willing and able to do this integrating and therefore willing and able to keep them alive (Chapter 4). Relations between practices take different forms – some collaborative, some competitive, some weak, some strong. Whatever form they take, such relations matter for the trajectories of the elements and individual practices of which composite bundles and complexes of practice are made (Chapter 5). Finally, the connections involved, between elements and practices and between one practice and another, are maintained and reproduced through intersecting circuits of reproduction that have dynamic qualities of their own (Chapter 6).

REPRESENTING ELEMENTS AND PRACTICES

In constructing this scheme we have made a number of breathtaking simplifications. One of the most striking is the contention that practices are composed of just three generic elements. Has this radical reduction been vindicated by what it has enabled? What have we contributed by taking this step? We come back to the more complicated challenge of conceptualizing elements in a moment but one obvious development, at least as regards more classically *social* theories, is our inclusion of materiality as a constitutive element of practice. Though barely mentioned by Giddens (1984), artefacts, technologies and infrastructures feature in Schatzki's account not as parts of practice, but as aspects of 'arrangements' to which practices are tied (2010b: 135). By going further and incorporating materiality as an element, not as a feature of arrangement, setting or environment, we have taken Latour's contention that material is the very 'stuff out of which socialness is made' (Latour, 2000:

113) rather literally. This does not mean we have gone along with all other aspects of actor network theory, but in taking this approach we have been able to build on the work of those who have written about how objects script practices and about how they act as media of storage and circulation (see Chapter 3, 'The life of elements').

The more challenging issue, though, is whether it makes sense, in general terms, to think of practices as integrations of elements and to then group these into three impressively broad categories. In developing this approach we took our inspiration from Reckwitz and from his suggestion that practices consist of interdependent relations between elements including 'forms of bodily activities, forms of mental activities, "things" and their use, a background knowledge in the form of understanding, know-how, states of emotion and motivational knowledge' (2002: 249). In working with these ideas and using them to understand how practices circulate and change, we have taken endless liberties with the categories of materiality, meaning and competence. We have classified cast-iron stoves, skateboards, ink, infrastructures, bicycles and wing-mirrors as material elements as and when it suits us, paying little or no attention to their different and distinctive qualities. Our treatment of meaning and competence has been no more systematic. Accordingly, states of emotion have been folded into 'meaning', a term that also encompasses the symbolic significance of participation. Our justification is that however slippery it might be, this *analytic* strategy has allowed us to develop a method of thinking about the dynamics of practice, starting from first principles. By treating elements as building-blocks of practice, we have been able to identify emergent patterns and connections and say something about how these are made. In addition, the language of elements has allowed us to describe processes of transformation, diffusion and circulation and to extend theories of practice in these directions.

In order to track the careers of practices as they develop over time, we have had to make other simplifying moves. In particular, we have had to figure out what we are going to count as 'a practice'. One response is to treat practices as anything that practitioners themselves take to be such. This helps limit the field, but it does not solve the problem entirely. To describe the evolution of practices over time, for example, to show how 'driving' emerged from horse-riding and engineering, we had to make our own judgements about what to count. In Chapter 4 we took note of Schatzki's advice on this topic and took heed of his suggestion that 'where multiple mutations are accompanied by continuities in other components, a practice lives on' but that 'when changes in organization are vast or wholesale, or a practice's projects and tasks are simply no longer carried out, former practices expire' (2002: 244). But in the end it was we who determined how terms like 'vast' and 'wholesale' were to be interpreted. Others might come to different conclusions, and all such judgements are open to debate. Making them is, nonetheless, an essential part of conceptualizing stability and change.

Theories of practice are commonly thought to deal better with routine reproduction than with innovation. And this is to some extent true, especially for those who focus on the details of doing and on moments of enactment. From this point of view, 'a practice represents a pattern which can be filled out' (Reckwitz, 2002: 250): in short, it provides a template in terms of which actions are adjusted and calibrated. However, this is not the only way to go. Throughout this book we have been keen to build on the observation that not all enactments of practice are consistent or faithful and that each performance is situated and in some respect unique. In addition, in some small way each enactment changes the elements of which practices are made. By describing both the persistence and the mobility of materials, meanings and competence we have been able to show how the contours of practices-as-entities evolve (even when practitioners and performances are separated in space and time) and how practices relate to each other.

CHARACTERIZING CIRCULATION

In our account, elements simultaneously figure as ingredients of practices and points of connection between them. Though not usually framed in quite this way, parts of this argument are already well established. For example, numerous studies suggest that technologies and artefacts 'script' bodily performance and the types of competence required to produce configurations that work (Akrich, 1992). This is much the same as saying that objects act as vectors or carriers of other elements of practice. Since practices-as-performances are culturally and historically situated, elements are unlikely to be integrated in identical fashion in every setting (Shove and Pantzar, 2005). Even so, we have argued that it is useful to think about how elements travel and to consider the implications and consequences of these trajectories for the chances that relevant sets of meanings, materials and competences might coincide (such that practices might be reproduced), and for how these elements are distributed (and thus for who might qualify as an actual or potential practitioner).

In Chapter 3 we suggested that elements differ systematically in how they circulate (in lorries and wagons, through media representation, instruction manuals etc.) and in their capacity to persist beyond the life of the practices in and of which they were once a part. In discussing these themes we noticed that material objects may become stranded when forms of knowledge associated with them disappear. When this happens, artefacts continue to exist but not as elements of living practices. This is relevant in that our earlier proposition – that practices consist of integrations of existing elements – supposes that elements are somehow 'out there' waiting to be combined. However strange it might sound, the idea that we are surrounded by momentarily disconnected elements also helps in understanding situations in which variants of practices past are resurrected and reinstated not in exactly the same form, but in a form similar enough that they are recognizably related. We have already commented on this with respect to the resurgence of cycling in some countries but not others: an example we develop further in Chapter 8.

Discussion of these aspects and of the recursive relation between practices-as-performances and practices-as-entities allowed us to consider dynamic processes often overlooked in more bounded, more localized studies of situated enactment. We adopted a similar method, again focusing on the making and breaking of links, in showing the competitive, transformative and convergent ways in which practices relate to each other.

COMPETITION, TRANSFORMATION AND CONVERGENCE

Historical accounts of innovation, including those informed by 'multi-level' perspectives (Geels and Schot, 2010) frequently emphasize competitive battles, typically for market share. In analyses of this kind the fate of an incoming sociotechnical arrangement depends on its ability to survive in a selection environment defined and ordered around incumbent systems. We have used similar ideas, also invoking ecological metaphors, in our representation of how practices compete with each other. To the extent that time spent in the garden is not time spent in the living room, television viewing really did vie with gardening for cohorts of committed carriers. More recently, surfing the Internet and related forms of computer-based work and play appear to have taken time away from the television in particular. Narratives of replacement and substitution are sometimes sufficient, but patterns of emergence and transformation are frequently shaped by other, coexisting, overlapping forms of interdependence. As we showed, practices may also become dominant through more subtle processes of partial colonization, hybridization and cross-referencing.

Chapter 5 demonstrated the importance of these relations for the trajectories of individual practices and for the formation of more extensive bundles and complexes of practice. This is not a new insight, but in teasing out relevant forms of co-existence and comparing these with stickier forms of co-dependence we began to distil the types of connection involved. As part of this exercise we noticed that spaces like offices, homes and cities are of consequence for the lives of individual practices, for their distribution and for their capacity to develop over time. In permitting distinctive conjunctions and in favouring some but not other forms of association, places are more than contexts or settings in which performances are enacted. In certain situations, co-location results in new hybrid forms: novel practices emerge. Some of these synchronous associations are short-lived, but others set new trains of path-dependence in motion. For example, aspects of surfing (the board, the ability to balance) and roller-skating (the wheels) came together in skateboarding, a hybrid combination that has influenced the development of snowboarding (snowboarding is thus a blend of skateboarding, skiing and surfing). In describing how such interconnections come about in these and in other cases, we showed how traces of the past are inscribed in the patterns of the present and hence how practices connect through the course of human history.

REPRODUCING ELEMENTS, PRACTICES AND RELATIONS BETWEEN THEM

In writing about the lives of practices and practitioners we drew attention to the fact that there is no break in the stream of daily life: no moment when social arrangements start over afresh. Each 'new' combination of elements and practices is in some sense an emergent outcome of those that went before. Exactly how this pans out depends on forms of hybridization and reconfiguration of the type described above, and on related cycles of accumulation and path dependence. These are crucial for the emergence of 'dominant projects' and more extensive complexes capable of structuring the course that other practices take. In Chapter 6 we sought to describe the 'circuits of reproduction' through which elements relate to practices, and through which individual practices relate to bundles and complexes of practices, and we identified some of the forms of feedback involved. This led us to wonder, more speculatively, about whether the types of circuitry involved might not also have an emergent life of their own.

It is usual to argue that practices simultaneously constitute and are constituted by the ongoing enactment of daily lives and social structures. In this book we have tried to show *how* this occurs. In the process we have worked with a limited vocabulary, mobilizing stripped-down interpretations of elements, practices and practice complexes. This method has allowed us to identify and discuss processes of circulation, transformation and accumulation and provide a fuller sense of how structuration proceeds.

Throughout we have taken *practices and their reproduction/transformation* as our primary topic of concern. This does not mean we have ignored questions of agency or the part that practitioners play, but it does mean we have approached them from a particular point of view. In effect, we have consistently viewed people as the carriers of practice, a strategy that might seem to reduce the role of the human subject to that of an automaton. This is far from true. Since practices are, in fact, changing all the time it is evidently wrong to think of carrying as a passive process. There are two aspects to this. First, we have repeatedly made the point that practices are *active* integrations of elements, and that these integrations are inherently dynamic. So although it is frequently useful to think of practices capturing their carriers, not all prove to be faithful or reliable servants. Understanding how local variations of performance and enactment accumulate and persist is an essential part of understanding the dynamics of practice. Second, in our analysis there is nowhere to go outside the world of practice. One consequence, then, is that human agency is loosely but unavoidably contained with a universe of possibilities defined by historically specific complexes of practice. It is in this sense that practices make agency possible, a conclusion that is not at all incompatible with the related point that practices do not exist unless recurrently enacted by real-life human beings.

In the next parts of this chapter we explore the implications of this approach for representations of time and space. This is an important task in that materials, meanings and competences are not integrated in the abstract: practices, the outcomes of such integrations, happen somewhere and at some time. Similarly, the elements of practice are not equally distributed around the globe, nor do they last for ever. These details of when and where are relevant for understanding how past patterns and trajectories have a bearing on the future. That much is clear, but how are we to conceptualize the relation between space, time and practice? Should we view space and time as resources for which practices compete, in effect treating them as additional elements? Alternatively, would it make better sense to think of space and time as coordinates in terms of which the location of a practice might be described and plotted? Or should we go along with Schatzki's interpretation of activity timespace (Schatzki, 2010b) as something that is forged in the moment of doing, and through which past and future are integrated? In his formulation, 'time and space are inherently related constitutive dimensions of action and that the happening of action is the opening – or coming to be – of these dimensions: the opening of timespace' (2010b: xi). The following paragraphs explore these options first with respect to time, and then to space. In many ways this is a silly thing to do: space and time cannot be split apart. However artificial it might be, separate discussion of each is nonetheless revealing with respect to the reproduction and transformation of elements, practices and practice complexes.

TIME AND PRACTICE

If we were to look back through previous chapters we would come across different methods of representing temporal aspects of practice. In this section we revisit four such framings, first representing time as a finite resource for which practices compete. This approach supposes that the fate and future of different practices depends on how practitioners spend their days. The idea that minutes devoted to one practice cannot be invested in another is consistent with contemporary interpretations of clock-time, or objective time. We toyed with this approach when totting up the total number of person hours that practices might capture, doing so by multiplying the number of practitioners (world human population) by the number of waking hours each practitioner has available. Some practices take longer to perform than others, and some require precisely timed sequences of attention (*timing* and not just time are important), but in very crude terms, it is possible and sometimes useful to present practitioner-time as a necessarily limited, inherently finite resource, the allocation of which reflects the relative dominance of some practices over others, and which is consequently important for what might happen next.

There are other ways in which objective time, in the sense of passing hours, matters for the enactment of practices. Our second framing of the temporal aspects of practice came into view when we turned our attention from rivalries between practices as competitors for time, to the daily experiences of an individual practitioner. For any one individual, enacting a practice is a matter of weaving it into an existing rhythm and of honouring temporal injunctions inscribed in concepts of proper performance. For example, it is usual to eat breakfast in the morning, to

shower on a daily basis and devote a full 90 minutes to a game of football. These demands, again measured in hours and minutes, are important for how appointment diaries are organized and filled and for the
more-or-less deliberate scheduling of 'hot' and 'cold' spots in the day
(Southerton, 2003). In theory, everyone has access to the same number
of hours in a day, but for some people their time is simply not their own.
In the language of practice, for one reason or another they are bound to
carry specific practices, the enactment of which limits their scope to do
very much else. These are familiar situations. Once commitments to
family or to work-related practices are established, many other practices
are simply blotted out from the field of possibility.

Even so, the notion that practices compete for time does not do justice
to the intricate forms of interweaving involved. Nor does it help in
understanding how new practices are inserted into complex, variously
flexible sequences. The rapid and spectacular success of texting arguably
relates to the ease with which it colonized moments occurring between
or during the performance of other practices. This example suggests
overlapping rhythms of daily life structure innovations in practice, but
as we explain in a moment, these temporal rhythms are not abstract
patterns. They are themselves formed of related, co-existing practices.

Whether outcomes of brute competition or of subtler modes of symbiosis, sequencing and scheduling are important for the conduct of
practices-as-performances. However, if we are to think about how
practices-as-entities endure, we need to introduce our third framing of
the temporal aspects of practice. We have repeatedly made the point
that if practices are to persist they need to be recurrently performed. Yet
moments of enactment are not usually continuous: indeed, most are
spread out over time. This begs the question of how practices 'persist'
when they are not actually happening. We have argued that this durability depends on the parallel persistence of requisite elements (materials,
meanings, competences) and on cohorts of practitioners willing and able
to integrate these elements and in so doing enact the practice over again.
It is for this reason that we concentrated on the 'lives' of elements and
on their ability to lie dormant between and beyond occasions in which
they are actively integrated in practice. As described in Chapter 3, elements of meaning, materiality and competence bridge between instances

of performance. In this they have a dual role: connecting practices in objective time and in the same move structuring the way in which 'time' is experienced and organized within society.

When we turn from objective time to a discussion of how days and hours are experienced, practices and elements appear in a new light. Our fourth framing of the temporal aspects of practice is the most radical in that it suggests that rather than competing for time, time is something that practices 'make'. Some practices, like baking bread, have temporal qualities that are hard to avoid: the dough has to rest and rise before the bread goes in the oven, and when in the oven it needs to cook for just so many minutes. This temporal sequence is born of the practice itself. The same applies to complex patterns of synchronization like those generated by practices the effective accomplishment of which demands the co-presence of many people. There is, in addition, a sense in which time is known and experienced through the performance of practice, hence 'the week-end is the week-end precisely because we do things on Saturdays and Sundays that we don't do on Mondays and Tuesdays' (Shove, 2009: 19). Put simply, experiences of time are part and parcel of the experience of practice.

In this brief review we have singled out contrasting methods of conceptualizing the relation between practice and time. We began by representing time as something for which practices compete and went on to identify temporal schedules as patterns into which practices are inserted. We then contended that elements allow practices to endure over time and concluded by arguing that practices in some sense make time. These positions are not as incompatible as they might at first appear. The fact that we have moved between all four in the course of this short book is symptomatic of an attempt to analyse the dynamics of social practice by interrogating the different parts of our model (elements, practices, relations between practices, practitioners-as-carriers) one at a time.

When reassembled, these various pieces of argument allow us to see how the temporal infrastructures of society, such as of the working day, the working week or the weekend, are made and reproduced through the fine detail of what people do. Societal rhythms are defined by the recurrent scheduling and sequencing of specific practices and, over the longer run, changing patterns of daily life reflect the dynamics of social practice. Grand historical shifts in temporal organization such as those explored by Thompson (1967) or Elias (1969) can be recast in these terms. From this perspective, the temporal structuring of work, production and communication can be understood as an outcome of incremental shifts in successive performances of practices, shifts which are themselves shaped by relations between one practice and another and by the circulation and transformation of elements on which all depend.

SPACE AND PRACTICE

The details of where practices happen are also relevant in thinking about how they change and diffuse. So what is this spatial aspect and how have we represented it? A review of previous chapters would again confirm that our working method has led us to switch between different positions, sometimes viewing space as a resource, other times as a representation of geographical location and often as a concept that is itself an outcome of practice. To some extent these treatments run parallel to the conceptualizations of time described above, but the correspondence is not exact. In describing some of the differences at stake we touch on related issues of inequality as these play out in the distribution and circulation of elements and practices.

In the previous section we began by talking about practitioner-time as a resource for which practices compete. We now ask whether the same applies with respect to space. This proves to be a tricky question. In Chapter 4 we calculated that each day affords something like 108 billion person-hours theoretically available for capture by the totality of practice-entities reproduced in the world today. Since practices also take place in, and consequently require, space we might take a similarly straightforward approach. The vast majority of practices happen on dry land and are therefore distributed across 149 million km^2 of the earth's surface. Although this is an impressive figure it does not take a moment to realize that it is not a very useful point of reference. Since practices need practitioners, it would make sense to exclude tracts of unoccupied land. Some further calculation would then be required to determine the extent of 'viable practice space'; that is, the space in which practitioners could potentially enact practices in the finite amount of time available to them.

The chances of arriving at any such estimate are slim. For a start, access to 'viable practice space' is likely to vary from one practitioner to the next. This works in different ways. Densely populated sites, where there are many practitioners available for capture, tend to generate spatial constraints that limit the range of practices by which those many practitioners might be captured. Depending on where they are located, practitioners have more or less space available to them. But the significance of this constraint varies in that certain practitioners have resources that allow them to escape the limitations of space which afflict others.

For these reasons we cannot pin down the contours of available territory. Nor can we readily determine the spatial 'needs' of any one practice. If we set aside secondary spatial requirements like those associated with the production of requisite elements (materials, meanings and competences), it might be possible to conclude that the area required for day-dreaming is smaller than that needed for playing a game of football or growing crops. Literal calculations of this kind fail to take into account other space-related features, like the need for a *level* playing field, but there are other, still more challenging problems ahead, in that certain practices transform zones of available space. Systems of automobility have, for example, enlarged what we might think of as the global resource of 'total potential access to space-suited-to-the-enactment of practices'. In effect, driving has simultaneously taken space, in the form of roads, parking areas and so on, *and* made it possible for more people to do more things in more places than ever before. To complicate matters further, the spaces that practices require and occupy are often overlain and interwoven, having only vague boundaries.

We clearly need to back away from the project of specifying the spatial requirements of practice on a global scale and from thinking about competition in these terms. There are, however, numerous situations in which practices do seem to vie for space. In many urban areas playing in the street has been displaced by driving. In situations like these, streets have become sites of transport, not of leisure. But as this sentence indicates, space is itself defined by what goes on with in it, hence stretches of tarmac turn from being playgrounds to roads when used in different ways. This is important at the level of performance, and crucial for where practices are enacted. But again we need to go further if we are to show how the situated ordering of performances like these relate to the distribution of practices-as-entities.

In writing about time we wrote about how practices endure between periods and moments of performance. In response we pointed to the ongoing persistence of elements and of populations willing to integrate these elements in more-or-less consistent combinations in the future. The question we now face is how practices 'travel', whether by edging into adjacent territory or by jumping from one spot to another. In Chapter 3, we concluded that what looks like the diffusion of practices-as-entities is better understood as a consequence of their re-enactment in multiple sites. In short, practices do not literally travel, but elements certainly do. The potential for re-enactment across the world consequently depends on the availability of requisite elements. As we have seen, materials, meanings and forms of competence circulate in characteristically different ways. Whilst some are unscathed by these journeys, others are typically transformed in the process of translation/transportation. For the moment, though, the main point is that the diffusion of practices depends on the distribution of elements and on who has access to them.

Space fits into this discussion in four distinct but related ways. First, elements cannot travel everywhere. Potential journeys are variously constrained by physical limits and by the social geography of pre-existing practices and the traditions, meanings, material infrastructures and competences associated with them. These constitute uneven landscapes of possibility. For example, complex and demanding forms of expertise cannot be grafted on in the absence of appropriate background knowledge. Likewise, electricity has become an essential pre-condition for the effective operation of many material elements and hence for the enactment of practices that depend on these technologies. The circulation of elements is, in addition, structured by the scope and range of an array of mediating networks including those of communication and related forms of physical and virtual mobility.

The second, more complicated point has to do with the co-constitution of space and practice. As they travel and when they are integrated in new sites, combinations of elements (and the practices they enable) re-make space. In the example above, playgrounds become thoroughfares. Similar processes play out at many scales, not least because practices themselves combine to form more extensive bundles and complexes. In theory, one might use these ideas to describe trends like those of 'Westernization'. At one level, the adoption of 'Western' practices depends on access to the materials required. In a study of how air-conditioning came to Japan, Wilhite writes about the materialization of a Western way of life, and about the styles of clothing, drink (whisky) and interior decor required (Wilhite et al., 1997). However, this is only part of the story in that the adoption of such practices re-defines the spaces in which they are enacted. As 'Western' styles, broadly defined, become integrated into daily life, places like Tokyo qualify for inclusion in a list of world cities, these being cities defined by the recurrent reproduction of standard lifestyles/practice complexes.

Our third closely related observation is that in so far as places are defined by practices, communities of practice, including those that are in objective terms widely dispersed, arguably inhabit the same practice-space. From this point of view, using the Internet to play poker with people around the world is not a matter of overcoming space but of creating and reproducing a distinctive but distributed 'place'. In Chapter 5 we considered situations in which the co-location of practices proved to be relevant for pathways of future development (we wrote about offices, homes and kitchens). We can now see that more virtual forms of 'co-location' – that is, sharing similar practice-space – might have similar consequences.

Finally, the conclusion that space and time are produced and reconstituted through the enactment of practices is significant in that the consequences of such enactments accumulate and persist in the temporal-spatial fabric of society. As driving and flying reconstitute space and time around them, they help embed the future inevitability of driving and flying. Both become necessary if life is to go on within the reconfigured spatialities and temporalities these practices have engendered.

As with our discussion of time, we contend that these different representations are not in conflict: sometimes it does make sense to talk of competition for space, or to consider the unequal distribution of spatial 'resources'. In a simple way, those who own a lot of land have access to practices denied to those who do not. This does not prevent us from going along with Schatzki's account of space and time being co-present in the moment of activity or from considering the longer-term consequences of such moments for the specification of what places are, or for the emergence of shared understandings of what goes on within them. So yes, time and space are present together in the moments when practices are enacted as performances; yes, such performances are likely to demand a share of objective time (minutes, hours), and sufficient practice-space in order to happen at all; and yes, again, practices constitute meanings of time and space that are in turn relevant for the distribution of such practices, and hence for the accumulation and circulation of the elements of which actual and potential practices are made.

In conclusion, space and time are not elements equivalent to those of materiality, meaning and competence. They do not circulate in their own right, nor are they shared and stored in the same way. Equally, spatial and temporal coordinates do not merely define the settings and scenes in which practices are enacted. Arrangements of time and place are structured by past practices and are themselves relevant in structuring future pathways of development and/or diffusion. In this role they act like elements in that they constitute media of aggregation and storage, holding the traces of past practice in place in ways that are relevant for the future, and for the perpetuation of unequal patterns of access.

DOMINANT PROJECTS AND POWER

We have not explicitly engaged with big debates about the rise of capitalist society or with questions of social and economic power. But that does not mean that these are in any sense absent from our analysis of

the dynamics of social practice. In this last part we bring issues of inequality and access to the fore and comment on how these figure in our
representation of elements, practices and relations between them.
Chapter 4 ended with a rather brief discussion of what Pred (1981)
refers to as 'dominant projects', these being complexes of practice that
orient the ways in which people spend their time and the priorities
around which their lives are organized. For Pred, systems of class and
power are sustained through the social reproduction of dominant
projects. In his account, and in ours, such projects become dominant
and remain so because they are enacted at many levels at once, being
reproduced through the daily paths and the life paths of individuals and
through the parallel reproduction of institutions, including those of
work and family life. From this point of view, states and economies are
constituted through the recurrent performance of some but not other
practices.

Though not yet put in so many words, the emergence, persistence
and disappearance of practices (guided and structured by dominant
projects) generates highly uneven landscapes of opportunity, and
vastly unequal patterns of access. To return to the example of automobility, one consequence of the dominance of car-driving as a practice is
that spaces once available to the practitioner-carriers of cycling and
walking are increasingly occupied by a relatively affluent minority and
the vehicles in which they travel. Different individuals stand to gain or
lose as certain practices take hold and as others disappear. With automobility, as with much else, the emergence of practice complexes is of
direct consequence for shifting distributions of goods and bads within
society.

Trajectories of practices, some dominant, some disappearing, are
also significant for the specification and distribution of relevant forms
of material, meaning and competence. Those who have the means to
engage in valued social practices are in an especially privileged position in that it is they who contribute to the direction in which such
practices develop. The specification of relevant elements and their cir-
culation/distribution are in this respect intimately connected (Bourdieu,
1984). Meanwhile, those who are socially excluded are those who
lack the means to become carriers of practices deemed essential for

effective participation in society. Exactly what this entails is itself an outcome of the changing constellations of practices that constitute the social world.

We have consistently argued that links and connections between elements and practices are rooted in past inequalities and constitutive of similar patterns in the future. However, we have not yet paid attention to deliberate or wilful attempts to bring new practices into being or to kill them off for good. On this topic, Burke's discussion of making markets for soap provides a useful point of reference. It does so in that Burke highlights the role of key companies and the importance of alliances built with church and state, all enlisted in the project of generating new concepts of dirt. As Burke (1996) describes, this was an essential step in establishing the need for equally new practices of washing, the effective accomplishment of which depended on the Lifebuoy and Lux brands of soap. His is a complicated and revealing narrative in that it operates on different levels. On the one hand, it describes the ambitions and efforts of a handful of powerful actors. On the other hand, it shows how their actions changed the texture of social and economic interaction and in so doing changed the manner in which power is exercised. In brief, Burke (1996) argues that in cultivating practices of personal hygiene in Zimbabwe, the organizations involved were instrumental in establishing the very idea of market transactions. In effect, they changed the types of connections and the forms of linkage through which exchanges took place, and as such were of importance well beyond the realm of personal hygiene.

Our account is similar in locating sources of power not (only) in the resources and capacities of individual actors but in the circuits of reproduction through which elements and practices are brought together and by means of which they are pulled apart. In these respects, the picture of power presented in Chapter 6 is decidedly Foucauldian.

At different points through the book we deal with issues of dominance, accumulation, access and the circuitry of reproduction, but in the end our most basic and most obvious contribution is to take practices as the central unit of enquiry and change. This is a critical step in that it structures the way we think about what people do and about how practices change and how they stay the same.

As we noticed in Chapter 1, public policies, including those designed to promote sustainability, routinely take individuals to be the source of change; but what if people are better understood as the carriers of practice? If we take this conclusion seriously, the challenge of promoting less resource-intensive ways of life is at heart a matter of reconfiguring the practices of which society is made. The question is then whether policy makers can intervene in the dynamics of social practice, and if so how, on what basis and with what chance of success?

8

PROMOTING TRANSITIONS IN PRACTICE

In exploring the potential for developing practice-oriented approaches to public policy, we move out from the shelter of the previous chapters and from the protected space they have provided for cultivating the different stages of our account. In this chapter we confront a more rugged environment in which theories, like practices, compete with each other for advocates and carriers.

When moving into this territory, and when thinking about what it means to produce useful and relevant research, it is important to remember that social theories do not lead directly to prescriptions for action. In allowing us to understand the world in a particular way, they are nonetheless relevant for how policy agendas and problems are defined and framed and for the kinds of intervention that are deemed possible, plausible or worthwhile. It is in this spirit that we approach the task of characterizing the policy relevance of practice theory, broadly defined. Taking *practices* rather than the individuals who carry them as the core unit of analysis makes sense in terms of social theory, but what does it mean for policy, or for deliberate efforts to intervene in what Giddens (1984: 3) describes as the constitution of society?

On the face of it, one would expect strategies informed by theories of practice to follow a different course to those that view behaviour change as an outcome of personal preference. This is so in that contrasting models of the social world are likely to produce different ideas about the scope and role of policy intervention. There are exceptions, some of which we discuss below, but policy making is typically informed by concepts from economics and psychology (e.g. theories of planned behaviour, models of rational economic action, representations of habits as drivers of behaviour etc.) and is for the most part untouched by developments in sociological theory. The purpose of this chapter is to show what practice-oriented policy might actually involve.

CLIMATE CHANGE AND BEHAVIOUR CHANGE

We focus on climate change policy for two related reasons. First, climate change arguably represents 'the greatest long-term challenge facing the human race' (Blair, 2006: 4). Second, it is challenging precisely because the prospect of any effective response depends on changing social practices. As Grin et al. put it, profound transformations of the type required 'involve, by definition, changes in established patterns of action as well as in structure (which includes dominant cultural assumptions and discourses, legislation, physical infrastructure, the rules prevailing in economic chains, knowledge infrastructure and so on)' (2010: 2). In other words, transitions are needed not only in the efficiency with which contemporary standards of living are met, but also in the bundles and complexes of practices of which daily lives are made.

In the first part of this chapter we consider the social-theoretical foundations of national and international strategies to promote 'pro-environmental behaviour'. As recent reports reveal, the policy task is generally defined as that of encouraging households to do their bit by consuming differently, reducing waste, using less energy, leaving the car at home, cycling more and eating lower-impact diets (Sustainable Consumption Round Table, 2006; DEFRA, 2008; Prendergast et al., 2008; United Nations Environment

Programme, 2008). This focus on consumer behaviour and lifestyle reso-nates with a political philosophy in which government's role is cast as that of 'finding intelligent ways to encourage, support and enable people to make better choices for themselves' (UK Cabinet Office, 2010: 8) and is consistent with a distinctly behavioural approach to policy making summed up here in a report from the UK's Institute for Government:

> [M]any of the biggest policy challenges we are now facing – such as the increase in people with chronic health conditions – will only be resolved if we are successful in persuading people to change their behaviour, their lifestyles or their existing habits.
>
> (Institute for Government, 2009: 1)

There is quite some debate about how far governments could or should go in 'editing' choices and manipulating individual ambitions and desires (Jones et al., 2010; O'Neill, 2010). Such discussions circle around a number of tougher questions about the legitimacy of state involvement in shaping preferences, encouraging deliberation, structur-ing options and 'nudging' individuals towards sustainability, or indeed any other policy goal (Thaler and Sunstein, 2009). Although there are real differences of opinion about the politics and propriety of state inter-vention, there is remarkably widespread agreement that what people do is in essence a matter of choice.

This is reproduced through repeated reference to a limited but hugely influential body of behaviour-change literature, including theories of planned behaviour (Ajzen, 1991) and variously rational models of need (Gatersleben and Vlek, 1998). Within this literature there are subtle dif-ferences of interpretation, for instance regarding the significance of con-text or the exact status of habit (Darnton, 2010). Yet the general pattern is one in which behaviour is taken to be a matter of choice, influenced by identifiable factors of which attitudes and beliefs are especially important.

The notion that behaviours mirror attitudes legitimizes extensive research designed to discover the character and extent of people's envi-ronmental values. In current policy circles, such knowledge is thought to be useful in distinguishing between target populations and in then customizing messages to appeal to the 'honestly disengaged', to those who want to be green but are 'stalled starters' and so forth (DEFRA, 2008). Strategies of this kind assume that a raft of 'behaviours', including driving, eating, washing and so on, are essentially similar in that the 'choices' people make about them reflect their environmental commitments, whether these be strong or weak. How these values translate into action is another matter, and many policy documents address the need to remove barriers, these being obstacles that seem to prevent people from acting according to their (green) beliefs.

This dominant paradigm of the 'ABC', in which A stands for Attitude, B for Behaviour and C for Choice (Shove, 2010), underpins two classic strategies for promoting more sustainable ways of life: one is to persuade people of the importance of climate change and thereby increase their green commitment; the second is to remove barriers obstructing the smooth translation of these values into action. Over the last few years, the language of motivators and barriers has been extended, behavioural economics has come into view, and there is increasing reference to the need for a more holistic approach. However, none of this has altered the basic outline of what remains a thoroughly individualistic understanding both of action and of change.

The following selection of questions extracted from a longer list on travel mode choice (i.e. on whether people choose to travel by car, bicycle, public transport etc.) illustrates key features of the kind of problem framing that follows:

a. what are the most influential drivers of behaviour affecting an individual's choice of mode of travel?
b. what is the role of infrastructure in encouraging and facilitating changes in travel-mode choice?
c. what are the latest developments in the evidence-base in relation to changing travel-mode choice and the implications of those developments for policy?
d. what are the most appropriate type and level of interventions to change travel-mode choice?

(House of Lords, Science and Technology Select
Committee, 2010: 2)

These questions, which form part of a call for evidence to be submitted to a UK House of Lords enquiry into behaviour change, make various assumptions about how the social world operates and how it can be known and changed. Whether people pick one mode of travel or another is evidently positioned as a matter of personal preference. Travel mode preferences are, in addition, taken to be determined by factors that can be identified and analysed in the abstract and without reference to specific cultural, geographical or historical settings. By implication, knowledge about the drivers of 'behaviour change' derived from studies of other areas of daily life, or from other countries, could and should be transferable.

There is nothing remotely unusual about this enquiry or about how it is framed. The topics identified reflect and sustain interpretations of the challenge of behaviour change and of possible responses to it that are widely reproduced and routinely taken for granted. Although popular and pervasive, these interpretations are quite at odds with theories of practice of the type developed in this book. Table 8.1 summarizes four points of difference, each discussed in a little more detail below.

Table 8.1   Behaviour and practice

	Theories of behaviour	Theories of practice
Basis of action	Individual choice	Shared, social convention
Processes of change	Causal	Emergent
Positioning policy	External influence on the factors and drivers of behaviour	Embedded in the systems of practice it seeks to influence
Transferable lessons	Clear: based on universal laws	Limited by historical, cultural specificity

Basis of action

Behavioural theories take the individual to be the primary agent of change. He or she may be influenced by 'social norms' or context, but the point is that such variables are thought to act as external pressures on what people do. A language of driving factors does not capture the extent to which forms of practical knowledge, meaning and competence are themselves forged and reproduced through the process of doing.

Processes of change

In policy documents and to a slightly lesser extent in the psychological literature on which they draw, there is a tendency to rely on cause-and-effect type explanations for why behaviours are as they are and for how they change. There is, as Geels and Schot put it, a fundamental difference between theories of variance, which explain 'outcomes as the product of independent variables acting on dependent variables' and theories of process, which take notions of path dependence seriously and which explain outcomes by tracing the stream of events through which a process unfolds. The more emergent concept of process allows that the unit of analysis 'may undergo metamorphosis over time and change meaning'. By contrast theories of variance necessarily suppose that 'the world is made up of fixed entities that maintain a unitary identity through time' (Geels and Schot, 2010: 79). This distinction is reproduced in how behavioural and practice-based theories conceptualize change.

Positioning policy

As hinted at above, contemporary efforts to promote pro-environmental behaviour position citizen consumers as the targets of government advice and encouragement. In representing their task as that of encouraging, enabling and helping citizens to do their bit, policy makers represent themselves as intervening from the outside, using different combinations of instruments – classically characterized as carrots, sticks and sermons – to remove barriers, give information and provide facilities such that individuals make 'better' choices for themselves.

This is consistent with a broadly behavioural approach, but if we conclude that the practices reproduced in any one society are outcomes of complex, essentially emergent processes over which no single actor has control, we have to think again about the actual and potential role of public policy.

Whether they recognize it to be so or not, policy makers are by implication themselves part of the patterns, systems and social arrangements they hope to govern: they do not intervene from the outside, nor do their actions have effect in isolation. In Arie Rip's words: 'instead of the heroism of the policy actor vis-à-vis the system there is a variety of actors and roles, and a distributed coherence which is self-organized. Some actors may contribute more to the self-organization than others, but there is no general rule' (2006: 87).

Co-evolutionary accounts of change do not deny the possibility of meaningful policy action: there are numerous routes through which policy, past and present, might be relevant and important, but the key insight here is that interventions have effect (some intended, some not) within and as part of the ongoing dynamics of practice. They do not work as abstract measures but as historically specific moves within a landscape of possibilities that is, in any case, always in transition. This argues for what Rip describes as a modest approach to policy, not based on a quest for control or an ambition to nudge the drivers of behaviour, but on a subtle and contingent 'understanding of the sociological and economic nature of the processes they seek to influence' (Grin et al., 2010: 207). Defined like this, policy making is not a matter of pursuing pre-defined outcomes by means of manipulating driving or obstructing factors. It is instead better understood as a more process-based 'succession of short and fairly rapid steps' involving sequences of 'trial-and-error' learning or 'serial adjustment', anchored in and never detached from the details and specificities of the practices in question.

Transferable lessons

Climate change policy makers expect to learn from efforts to change behaviour in other countries and in different areas of daily life: classic examples include programmes to persuade people to give up smoking or to start wearing seat belts. This expectation is consistent with the idea that behaviours are outcomes of identifiable factors and that it is therefore possible to identify, quantify and evaluate the merits of behaviour change techniques. By contrast, theories of practice draw attention to the historically and culturally specific trajectories of what people do, the details of which reflect distinctive accumulations of meaning, materiality and competence and the relative positioning of one practice with respect to others.

PRACTICE THEORY AND CLIMATE CHANGE POLICY

In combination these observations suggest that a practice orientation to policy would be one that, at a minimum, recognizes and works with and within processes that are essentially uncontrollable. This does not mean that policy making is inherently ineffective: far from it. It is true that since social practices are emergent, and their development unpredictable, there is little point in setting a target for practice change. After all, practices are always in transition. Nonetheless, certain policy interventions may increase the chances that more rather than less sustainable ways of life persist and thrive.

The position developed in Chapters 1 to 7 helps identify routes through which this might occur. In brief, policy makers and other actors, past and present, can and do influence: a) the range of elements in circulation; b) the ways in which practices relate to each other; c) the careers and trajectories of practices and those who carry them; and d) the circuits of reproduction. In the rest of this chapter we explore each of these avenues in turn and in the process outline the characteristics of an approach to policy making that builds upon a more systemic account of the social world and how it changes.

In showing how policy influences the dynamics of practice, we make use of cases that were not designed with this in mind. As these examples demonstrate, policy makers can and do influence trajectories of practice by accident, and as a side effect of programmes grounded in theories of rational action and choice. In bringing such examples together, and discussing the methodological implications of influencing processes of emergence, persistence and disappearance, we provide some practical illustrations of what a more overtly practice-oriented approach entails. We begin with the suggestion that policy makers might influence the elements of which practices are made.

Configuring elements of practice

> Climate change policymakers and visionaries should hunt down the elements that have the most negative impact upon carbon emissions across a whole group of practices. They should search out and design new elements that would support practices with fewer emissions. Policies would be directed not at bad behaviours, but at 'bad' elements.

This radical injunction, written on a Post-It™ note by an anonymous participant in a recent workshop on climate change, is not as fanciful as might at first appear. It turns the problem away from that of individual behaviour and prompts us to think about what 'bad' elements might be. Would candidates include electricity, meat, concepts of Westernization, the valuing of convenience, or competence in long-distance travel? It also makes us wonder: if 'bad' elements were not in circulation, what would become of the practices of which they are part?

The prospect of facilitating, or hindering, the availability and circulation of the elements (materials, meanings, competences), of which more and less sustainable practices are formed, does not feature prominently in contemporary climate change policy. But in areas like those of public health, there is a longer tradition of combining investment in infrastructures (sewerage systems, mains water) with campaigns instilling techniques like those of washing on a regular basis, along with ideas about what it is to be clean (Ogle, 1996; Melosi, 2000). Post-war urban planning provides many other examples of strategic efforts to provide the elements of which desired ways of living might be made. Tapiola, a Finnish town designed and built in the early 1960s, was inspired by Ebenezer Howard's vision of the model garden city (Howard et al., 1951); by Patrick Geddes's belief that spatial form could be used for social ends (1915), and by Lewis Mumford's ideas of technological progress (1939). In setting out streets, shops, homes and schools, Tapiola's planners were clear about what they wanted to achieve. Their aim was to create conditions in which children ran free, community was strong, interaction with nature was easy, and family life was close, harmonious and healthy. Ideological visions of the good life were inscribed and materialized in the smallest detail of kitchen design through to the distance between home and school (Hertzen and Spreiregen, 1971). Not everything went to plan, but there is no doubt that the ambition was to bring new social arrangements into being by providing the moral and material infrastructure around which they might develop. The idea that daily lives might be planned on such a scale, and with such precision, has fallen out of fashion and it is in any case clear that designers and nation-states have limited ability to control the circulation and flow of ideas about what it is to be modern or what a successful life entails. Many elements of practice circulate in ways that show scant regard for national borders. In addition, and in areas like food consumption or building design, global systems of provision are important in structuring diets and meals and in configuring the architecture of urban living. National policy makers can do only so much to promote or stem the transnational diffusion of materials, meanings and forms of competence, but as our next example illustrates, there are ways of intervening in how practices, in this case of keeping cool indoors, are constituted and in the forms of energy consumption they entail.

Air-conditioning technologies have made it possible to manipulate humidity, temperature and ventilation, and have been crucial in defining and diffusing standardized concepts of comfort and conventions of normal and appropriate clothing. Although vast quantities of energy are currently consumed in maintaining buildings at a steady 22 °C all year round, mechanical cooling has a relatively short history. In less than 70 years, methods of defining and calculating optimal indoor conditions, initially developed in northern Europe and the USA, have been appropriated and copied around the globe. This is important in that the projected energy costs of reproducing such conditions are massive: according to Sivak, 'the potential cooling demand in metropolitan Mumbai is about 24 per cent of the demand for the entire United States' (Sivak, 2009; Isaac and van Vuuren, 2009).

When sizing air-conditioning systems, architects and engineers make assumptions about what people wear, and in so doing they make use of a unit called the 'Clo'. One Clo is defined as the standard amount of insulation required to keep a resting person warm in a windless room at

70 °F (21.1 °C) (Gagge et al., 1941). This turns out to be 'the insulating value afforded by a man's underwear and a lightweight suit' (Fanger, 1973). The expectation that people will be wrapped in the thermal equivalent of pants, socks, shirt, trousers, jacket and tie is consequently embedded in the way that buildings and their heating and cooling systems are designed.

In thinking about how the demand for mechanical cooling has developed as it has, and about the energy this consumes, it is important to think about how the business suit, an outfit that has its origins in European fashion, has taken hold as the uniform of public life (Slade, 2009). Toby Slade, a fashion historian, suggests that the suit as we know it now integrates various traditions of Dutch Puritanism, French (post-revolutionary) aversion to ostentation and the rigours of British country life. It is true the suit has changed (waistcoats are no longer worn as a matter of course), and there have been some attempts at adaptation (the safari suit). But the general pattern is one in which this standard outfit has edged other more diverse, more traditional styles of clothing out of the frame. This process has not been studied systematically but Callaway's analysis of colonial influence and clothing is relevant (1992), as are efforts to document the suit's symbolic association with masculinity and with modern, Western and successful ways of life (McNeil and Karaminas, 2009). Whatever the secrets of the suit's success, these two related trajectories, one of clothing, the other of a standardized concept of comfort (achievement of which now requires energy intensive mechanical cooling), combine to sustain distinctly unsustainable arrangements. In hot climates, air-conditioning is adopted and routinely operated at temperatures designed to counter the effect of wearing levels of insulation afforded by the business suit.

Is it possible to break this vicious circle of energy demand and can environmental policy makers do so by redefining the *elements* of which practices of comfort are made and reproduced? In 2005 the Japanese government took such a step, introducing what is known as the 'Cool Biz' programme as part of an effort to reduce CO_2 emissions. The idea was simple: government buildings would not be heated or cooled between 20 and 28 °C, and occupants would be encouraged to remove jackets and ties in the summer and wear more in the winter (Warm Biz). In short, this was a concerted effort to change the *meaning* of normal clothing as a means of changing the technologies (levels of air-conditioning) and competences (of dress and of facilities management) involved in the routine enactment and effective accomplishment of office life. By most measures Cool Biz (the summer variant) has been spectacularly effective, resulting in estimated 1,720,000-ton reduction in CO_2 emissions (Team-6 Committee & Ministry of the Environment (Japan), 2007) and making a tangible difference to what men and women wear at work and, to a lesser extent, in the home.

This policy intervention appears to have successfully reconfigured the elements of practice, transforming collective conventions rapidly and on a significant if not societal scale. The Cool Biz programme worked on a number of fronts at once. The Ministry of Environment and their consultants made use of established marketing techniques to transform the *meaning* of smart and appropriate wear. The then prime minister, Mr Koizumi, and members of the cabinet were shown wearing loose-fitting short-sleeved outfits in formal settings. In 2006, the Ministry of Environment organized a much publicized fashion show during which ambassadors from various Asian countries made their way down the cat-walk in traditional, climatically appropriate wear. Successful business leaders were involved, the clothing industry responded to the challenge, and large department stores promoted especially designed garments under the Cool Biz name.

To have effect, these new styles had to be taken up in practice, and in the world of business, clothing is about more than insulation. A number of respondents, interviewed as part of a qualitative study of Cool Biz in daily life, described the complexities of putting these ideas into action. Some talked about especially difficult situations, like job interviews, in which the no-tie convention disrupted the normal semiotics of power. Others described frequent sartorial dilemmas: ties were required when meeting clients for the first time, but not on subsequent encounters. Looking back on the first few years of the Cool Biz programme, male office workers reported on a transition period in which they carried a tie around with them, stored in the pocket and ready for action should a clearly formal situation arise. By contrast, most of the women interviewed were simply relieved that the 'cold old days' were a thing of the past and that they were no longer obliged to wear light clothing in 'freezing' air-conditioned environments. Stories like these remind us that elements of meaning – including the meaning of office-wear, style and comfort – do not arrive fully formed but are reproduced and transformed in social situations that are already laden with significance.

Although not inspired by social theories of practice and not positioned as a rejection of unsustainable conventions imported from the West, Cool Biz appears to have changed expectations of indoor climates and of what it is acceptable to wear, steering both in a direction that reduces energy demand (De Dear, 2007). While influential at the level of fashion, Cool Biz has yet to be deeply embedded in policy thinking or in the infrastructures of design. Ironically, models of Japan's CO_2 emissions assume that buildings will be maintained at around 22–24 °C all year round, and there are so far no plans to revise building design guides in line with the assumption that indoor temperatures can and should range between 20 and 28 °C. More by accident than intent, Cool Biz nonetheless constitutes a fine example of how policy can reconfigure the elements of practice.

In this case the government focused on the meaning of clothing as a means of reducing the need for air-conditioning and the CO_2 emissions associated with it. From many points of view this was a method of quickly cutting energy consumption on a noticeable scale. It was also logical: why not remove jackets and ties and allow indoor temperatures to rise, and why not wear a bit more clothing and turn the heating down when it is cold? Thermal comfort researchers since have raised concerns about the loss of productivity and the tie industry has complained but, for the most part, the scheme has not threatened powerful established interests – for energy suppliers there are advantages in managing peak load. It is true that intervening with respect to clothing challenges complex and delicate processes of social interaction, order and propriety (Douglas, 1984), but these arrangements are perhaps more bounded and tractable than those of which entire systems of mobility or of diet are formed. In the next section we consider situations in which practices are more obviously embedded in evidently complex institutions and infrastructures.

Configuring relations between practices

In Chapter 5, 'Connections between practices', we wrote about how practices support and compete with each other, sometimes forming dense clusters or loose bundles that hang together in different ways across space and time. In that chapter, and in Chapter 2, 'Making and breaking links', we considered the types of connections that are made and broken as old practices disappear and new ones emerge. In climate change policy, and in literature exploring the potential for systemic innovation (Elzen et al., 2004), there is a tendency to focus on methods of stimulating and facilitating the breakthrough of more sustainable technologies. Rather less is said about the routes and pathways through which existing regimes and unsustainable practices break down, but in so far as practices vie for finite amounts of time, space, materials and 'carriers', this is also important in constructing lower carbon ways of life.

Before commenting on how policy makers might act to forge or break links between practices, we begin by describing the changing relation between systems of velo and automobility. This example allows us to catch sight of shifting populations of relevant elements and to speculate on the possibility of engendering a future system in which driving is significantly displaced by cycling. Cycling is now widely recognized as a practice that is good for the environment and for personal health: Sustrans claims that 2 kg of carbon are saved for every short journey made by bike (Sustrans, 2008). It is also a means of transport that used to be very much more widespread than it is today. In 1949 in the UK, an estimated '34% of all mechanized journeys were made by bicycle. Fifty years later that figure had fallen to 2%' (Times online, 2008). By any standards this is a spectacular decrease, representing a rapid and radical movement away from a lower carbon practice-complex.

Although this decline coincided with the rise of the car as an increasingly democratic means of personal mobility, the narrative is not one of simple substitution. As Geels explains, histories of driving and cycling are marked by extensive forms of symbiosis. The development of cycling laid the foundations for many of the elements on which the coming system of automobility depended (Geels, 2005), including aspects of infrastructure (road surfaces, production capacity) along with ideas and expectations of personal mobility. Sometimes symbiotic, sometimes competitive, the driving–cycling relationship is inherently dynamic. In the mid-1930s, when 20 per cent of men's journeys to work in the UK were made by bicycle, roads were relatively quiet, bikes were heavy, solid and widely available (Pooley and Turnbull, 2000). At that point, driving was still largely a pursuit of the elite and still associated with leisure. This switched around: as car driving became something for many and not just a few, cycling headed in the opposite direction. Cycling began to lose its meaning as a normal means of travel for all and became associated with leisure and with men. These observations suggest that related but not entirely symmetrical processes of innovation and disappearance continue to have effect today. In other words, past and present interaction is persistently relevant for the accumulation (or not) of material arrangements (roads, urban design) along with associated conventions, expectations, habits and routines, and hence for the terms on which cycling and driving relate to each other.

Whether cycling is characterized as slow, dangerous or effortful is not just a matter of personal opinion, but is instead related to the systemic configuration of this practice and of others in terms of which it is defined. For example, in the 1940s, and when compared to walking, cycling provided a fast means of covering extended distances. These qualities are relative, and when cycling takes place in environments designed around cars, or when daily routines involve travelling distances only made possible by the car, cycling is no longer speedy or convenient. In short, interpretations of cycling as a normal or an unusual thing to do depends on how riding is positioned within and by an interdependent network of social and material arrangements.

These ideas are useful in making sense both of the rapid decline of cycling in many European countries between the 1950s and 1970s and of its resurgence in some locations but not in others. According to Pucher and Buehler, 'the bike share of trips fell from 50–85% of trips in 1950 to only 14–35% of trips in 1975 in a range of Dutch, Danish and German cities'; however, during the mid-1970s, concerns about the environment and the quality of life led to 'a massive reversal in transport and urban planning policies' (2008: 496) and to variously concerted efforts to promote cycling. In some European countries, rates of cycling have increased sometimes by as much as 20 per cent since the mid-1970s, but in others, like the UK, the modal share has remained more or less unchanged at around 1 per cent for the last 40 years (Cabinet Office Strategy Unit, 2009).

This variation is intriguing: what Urry (2004) refers to as the 'system of automobility' is no less established in Denmark than in the UK. In these as in other countries, the petrol and steel car has been systematically locked into the organization of society. Cars have become progressively embedded through patterns of economic and suburban development and through the remaking of space and time in ways that demand and assume a relentless logic of automobility. In reflecting on the uneven revival of cycling across different countries and cities, de la Bruheze (2000) suggests that generic trends in automobility disguise important local variation in the extent and degree to which alternative regimes (including those of cycling) co-exist. In the Dutch case, the *persistence of relevant elements*, including meanings, competences and bicycle-related infrastructures, seems to have made it easier to reinstate cycling to at least some degree. By contrast, similar efforts have met with limited success in the UK, perhaps 'because bicycle use had declined too far' and because the 'material and social bicycle culture had disappeared' (2000: 4). This suggests that in some circumstances the elements of cycling-as-normal endure, but in dormant form, and that in others, it is not just that requisite links are temporarily broken but that vital elements have actually disappeared. In such settings:

> Attempting to reform technology without systematically taking into account the shaping context and intricacies of internal dynamics may well be futile. If only the technical components of a system are changed, they may well snap back into their earlier shape like charged particles in a strong electromagnetic field. The field also must be attended to; values may need to be changed, institutions reformed, or legislation recast.

> (Hughes, 1993 [1983]: 465)

For policy makers seeking to engender change, the two situations described above – one in which links are broken but relevant elements exist (as in Denmark and the Netherlands), the other (the UK) in which necessary elements are not (or no longer) in place – call for quite different forms of intervention. Yet other strategies would be needed if the task was to build elements and links from scratch.

This far we have discussed driving and cycling in order to draw attention to the changing relation between practices, to the potential for symbiotic as well as competitive relationships and to the consequences of past configurations for the accumulation, character and durability (or otherwise) of relevant elements. Since policy interventions take place within and not outside locally specific histories of practice, issues of *timing* are crucial.

In the Netherlands, the city of Groningen has been shaped by long-term mutually reinforcing policies of compact land-use planning, schemes to restrict car use and investment in cycling infrastructure. This history, and the fact that 40 per cent of local trips are currently made by bike, means that programmes designed to promote (yet more) sustainable personal transport have effect in a situation in which cycling is already a normal thing to do. This is not the case in London, where cycling now has only 1–2 per cent of modal share. The fact that policy makers encounter cycling at different moments in the practice's (local) career is important for the scope and potential impact of intervention. Various initiatives in London, including the congestion charge (introduced in 2003 – car drivers pay to enter the central London charging zone during certain hours of the day) and direct investment in bicycle routes, have coincided with rapid and recent recruitment to cycling in the city. Rates of cycling increased by at least 50 per cent between 2003 and 2007 and continue to grow. Although this is from a very low base, the sheer pace of change might imply that certain positive feedback effects are underway: that cycling is quickly becoming more normal as more normal people do it.

The prospect of deliberately engineering the demise of automobility and the rise of cycling as a newly dominant form might be a distant one, but in thinking about the potential for reconfiguring relations between practices, we have identified a number of key points. In so far as they make a difference, policy initiatives do so not in the abstract but to processes that already have a life of their own. Political opportunities for intervention, and the form these take, are emergent effects of the systems that policy makers seek to influence. Second, where such interventions reconfigure the relation between practices, for example systematically prioritizing bicycles over cars, they can set in train processes of positive feedback, the effects of which are unpredictable in terms of extent (e.g. regarding the scale of recruitment) and depth (e.g. how firmly new configurations become embedded). Third, and as mentioned above, it is important to attend to the disappearance and erosion of elements of undesirable practices, and to breaking the links which hold these arrangements in place. Finally, in thinking about the careers of practices and their carriers, it is evident that processes of defection are as crucial as those of recruitment, a topic to which we now turn.

Configuring careers: carriers and practices

In Chapter 4, 'Recruitment, defection and reproduction', we wrote about how practices maintain and lose their grip and how people become variously faithful and committed carriers. If practices are to survive they have to secure and maintain resources and practitioners willing and able to keep them alive. The question we now face is how policy makers influence these dynamics. There are various threads to follow: How are patterns of access and participation structured by policy? How do specific initiatives in climate change policy intersect with the careers of practices and practitioners? How does policy making shape networks and relationships through which practices are reproduced and carried?

At the most basic level, the probability of encountering and participating in different practices is itself structured by divisions like those of gender and social class. The suggestion that governments should enhance what Dahrendorf (1979) refers to as 'life chances' – meaning an individual's opportunity to maximize his or her talents – acknowledges these inequities of access and distribution, some of which are rooted in patterns of past advantage. This suggestion points to other also important questions about the range of practices to which people aspire, about what talents count and what it means to maximize them. For Bourdieu, the idea of habitus provides a means of bridging between the cumulative (and unequal) effects of past experiences, resources, dispositions and tastes, and the content and character of *future oriented* aspirations and opportunities (Bourdieu, 1984). Pred takes up this theme: 'through the operation of habitus the particular economic and cultural practices in which individuals of a given group or class partake appear "natural," "sensible," or "reasonable," even though there is no awareness of the manner in which those practices are either adjusted to other practices, or structurally limited' (1981: 8). In other words, definitions of valued pursuits, in relation to which interpretations of life chances make sense, are themselves outcomes of dialectical interaction between individual and institutional projects. These relations are critical in that 'social transformation and altered structural relations can only occur through the introduction, disappearance or modification of institutional projects' (1981: 17).

But what of the detail? How does the production of valued social practices proceed and how are dominant projects, some of which are much more resource intensive than others, configured? In Chapter 4 we introduced and discussed Pred's attempt to pin such processes down and to show how daily paths and life paths intersect with the trajectories of the social institutions of which they are a part. In that chapter we noticed that past performances are relevant for the accumulation of know-how and competence and for the changing meaning of participation, and that individual trajectories are, at the same time, ordered around collective projects.

What do these observations mean for policy makers and others seeking to promote more sustainable practices? Answers vary depending on the temporal and spatial scales we choose to consider. At the broadest, most 'macro' level, institutional projects are complex amalgams of past trajectories and current aims and aspirations, many of which are materially sustained and reinforced by the state. Investment in cycling infrastructures does not guarantee that cycling will capture willing carriers, but it does shape the distribution of requisite elements. Less obvious but no less important, governments have a hand in reproducing versions of normal and acceptable ways of life, and in configuring 'projects' that require specific patterns of mobility. The idea that parents should have a choice of schools has, for instance, generated more moving around than was the case when children went to the one that was closest to home. Other self-fulfilling conventions of need and entitlement are tacitly buried in plans and strategies for energy supply and in the design of resilient water infrastructures. In these cases, systems are planned and sized to cope with patterns of demand expected to follow from the mass reproduction of energy or water consuming practices. Such practices and associated 'standards of living' are, in effect, inscribed in how infrastructures are conceptualized and managed. Through arrangements like these, variously sustainable institutional projects are tacitly reproduced all the time, not at the forefront of explicit policy intervention but as part of the backdrop of taken-for-granted order: this being an order structured around historically specific bundles and complexes of practice. In regard to climate change, this argues for sweeping, systemic reviews of how different areas of public policy (education, health, family, work, leisure etc.) inadvertently but effectively reproduce unsustainable ways of life.

If we change scale and think about how specific policy interventions matter for what people do, other considerations come into view. As discussed in Chapter 4, the impacts of past and present forms of policy making are filtered through the life paths of individuals who begin from diverse starting points, and who belong to different generations. This is not just a matter of recognizing that programmes like Cool Biz catch people at different moments in their lives, and catch them as actual or potential carriers of specific practices. Although that is the case, the further issue is that conventions, in this case of clothing and cooling, are themselves dynamic. Cool Biz managed to recruit many carriers in a short space of time. In less than five years, running air-conditioning 'cold' and wearing a tie and jacket in the summer turned from being a normal to an exceptional thing to do. For some individuals, this was a disturbing, even threatening process, requiring them to abandon the habits of a lifetime. For others it was a relief: bringing institutional expectations into line with their own more casual approach. Out of many such trajectories, a new pattern has emerged. The meaning of 'normal' has been recalibrated in ways that are of collective as well as personal significance for present patterns of consumption.

The suggestion that practices might amplify or compete with each other (see Chapters 5 and 6) implies that, in general, policy makers would do well to consider parallel tracks that matter for the careers of the practices they seek to change. In some cases, as with Cool Biz, policies tap into social processes that are already underway. For a number of respondents, Cool Biz represented just one aspect of a trend towards more casual styles of conduct as well as of dress. In other situations, interventions 'catch' practices at different stages of stability and flux and in different states of association, one to another. Water is, for instance, used in the home as part of laundering, washing up, gardening, bathing and showering. At any one moment, some of these practices are more consistently reproduced than others. Over the last 30 years, the frequency with which people shower and wash their clothes has increased significantly. The idea of what a garden is, and hence the amount of watering it requires, is itself dynamic, but the point is that changes in this area are typically unrelated to what goes on behind the bathroom door. Finally, and as we saw in relation to commuter cycling in the UK, practices can persist for years without much change in what they entail or in the type and number of people involved.

The point here is that whether they are aware of it or not, policy makers intervene in processes that intersect, but that are also moving at different rates and scales. As Grin et al. put it, 'changing practices, structural change and exogenous tendencies occur and unfold parallel to each other and may sometimes interact so as to produce non-incremental change in practices and structures' (2010: 4). In an attempt to bring this feature to the fore, Geels and Schot refer to Braudel's characterization of three co-existing chronologies, these being:

a) structural history, associated with the study of geological, geographic, social and mental structures that change only glacially; b) conjunctural history, associated with the study of economic and demographic cycles with durations of decades rather than centuries; and c) eventful history, associated with the ephemera of politics and events reported in newspapers.

(Geels and Schot, 2010: 22)

This is useful in emphasizing the layering and mutual constitution of events and structures, and in reminding us that practices change at different rates (despite being linked). But we need to go further if we are to show how policy makers influence the means by which such links are made, and the circuits of reproduction involved.

Configuring connections

In Chapter 4 we noticed the importance of social networks through which practices circulate and develop and around which they are formed. By implication, the density and character of social bonds is important for how practices travel and for the populations they encounter and attract. Not all relevant interactions are face-to-face, and processes of recruitment and defection do not necessarily depend on geographical or social proximity. It is nonetheless possible that policy interventions, past and present, are cumulatively significant for the texture of the social fabric and hence for the routes through which recruitment and defection occurs. This is a plausible suggestion, but what does it mean for climate change policy: is there any clearly defined social form, or set of connections, that would of itself hasten the adoption of more rather than less sustainable practices?

Some argue that stronger local communities might have such effect. The Transitions Town movement makes this case, claiming that relocalization promises to result in a life that is 'more fulfilling, more socially connected and more equitable' (Brangwyn and Hopkins, 2008: 4). Meanwhile, others point to the liberating power of distributed, Internet-based relationships. Whatever conclusion they reach, analyses of this kind tend to separate 'networks', 'ties', 'bonds' and 'ligatures' from the practices and doings of which they are born, and from which they are in many respects inseparable. The observation that links are formed through doing specific practices argues for turning the problem around such that the policy question is not 'What sorts of social relations might enhance the circulation and adoption of more sustainable practices?', but rather 'What sorts of bonds and links might emerge from, and enable, the recurrent enactment of lower impact ways of life?'.

This re-framing does not mean that deliberate efforts to cultivate networks and partnerships are of no avail. However, it suggests that rather than concentrating on ways of engendering local community commitment to green ways of life, a move that typically involves conceptualizing community as a quasi-individual, complete with attitudes, beliefs and choices (see, for example, the Scottish Government's (2008) report on sustainable communities), policy makers would do better to study the changing contours of specific 'communities of practice' as conceptualized by Lave and Wenger (1991), and as discussed in Chapter 4. In this regard, and as illustrated in our discussion of Cool Biz, climate change policy makers have an obvious role in bringing existing actors together (i.e. businesses, manufacturers, marketing organizations, retail outlets) as part of a deliberate strategy to reconfigure the character and the distribution of the elements of which more sustainable practices *could be* made, and in seeking to break the ties that hold other less sustainable arrangements in place.

Much of the literature on 'transition management' (Rotmans et al., 2001; Berkhout et al., 2004; Smith et al., 2005) builds on the idea that policy influence occurs through pluralistic networks in which actors from 'government, the market and civil society participate in an interactive manner' (Loorbach and Rotmans, 2010: 197). This positions policy making not as an activity focused on the task of persuading individuals to act in line with agreed behavioural goals, but as a reflexive process of social learning and network building in which 'state actors rely upon non-state actors in the formulation and implementation of public policy' (Smith et al., 2005: 1498). Smith et al. contend that this is necessary in that transitions, including transitions toward sustainability, depend on the reconfiguration of multi-actor, multi-factor and multi-level systems that are dynamic, complex and interdependent.

From this perspective, effective policy making is about guiding processes of selection and variation, and about adapting to and reflexively monitoring emergent bundles and complexes of practice, as they develop. For Loorbach and Rotmans,

The very idea behind transition management is to create some kind of societal movement through new coalitions, partnerships and

> networks ... that allows for building up continuous pressure on the
> political and market arena to safeguard the long-term orientation
> and goals of the transition process.
>
> (Loorbach and Rotmans, 2010: 139)

There are reasons to be cautious about the politics of transition management (Shove and Walker, 2007). But for policy makers interested in promoting more sustainable practices, this literature illustrates the limits and possibilities of intervening in complex systems of culture (ways of thinking), practice (doing, routine, habit) and structure (organization) (Loorbach and Rotmans, 2010).

This discussion highlights three main points. First, policy interventions, like Cool Biz, depend on non-policy actors if they are to have effect. Second, such effects are inherently unpredictable – hence the conclusion that transition-style policy is not about delivering plans and advancing on ready-made goals, but about moving towards always-moving targets. Third, in the transitions literature, governments are thought to have a vital role in building networks and coalitions and in constructing partnerships that make the conditions of practice possible. To the extent that state actors do 'change behaviour' on any scale it is through these means, and not by dint of persuading individuals to modify their ways.

PRACTICE-ORIENTED POLICY MAKING

As represented in Chapters 1 to 7, elements, practices, bundles and complexes of practice and circuits of reproduction have interdependent, emergent lives of their own. In this analysis, people are somehow captured by the arrangements they sustain and to which they devote finite amounts of time, attention and resources. It is true, there are no reliable means of steering or governing transitions in practice: systemic forms of policy intervention only have effect when taken up in (and through) practice. Equally important, such effects are never stable, being always subject to ongoing reproduction.

However, these conclusions do not rule out the possibility of thought-ful, practice-oriented policy intervention. In this chapter we have explored the policy implications of different aspects of our argument: we have thought about how state actors influence the distribution and circulation of materials, competences and meanings and we have con-sidered their role in configuring relations between practices; in shaping the careers of practices and those who carry them, and in forging and breaking some of the links, relationships, networks and partnerships involved.

This exercise demonstrates that practice theories provide an intellec-tual base and a conceptual framework around which to build pro-grammes and policy interventions explicitly designed to address systemic challenges like those of engendering more sustainable routines and hab-its. The result is not a blueprint for practice-oriented policy, nor is it a template setting out exactly what to do. Such prescriptions are not to be expected: as we have already explained, the primary value of social theory is in framing the way the world is understood and how problems are defined.

It is at this level that the differences between conventional, ABC-type approaches to behaviour change and a practice-theory orientation are most obvious. These differences carry through to the kinds of knowl-edge thought relevant for promoting transitions in practice, and for definitions of relevant evidence and research (Shove, 2010). At the moment, large sums are spent surveying individual responses to batter-ies of attitudinal questions about the environment. This sort of informa-tion is of little value if the aim is to understand and potentially shape the range of practices of which contemporary society is formed. If that is the central question, other sorts of data and other styles of enquiry are required. These might include concerted and innovative efforts to quan-tify the growth of certain practices and the demise or transformation of others. If climate change calls for transitions of such a scale that conven-tions, standards, routines, forms of know-how, markets and expecta-tions need re-arranging across all domains of daily life, a further challenge is to determine how systemic moves in this direction might be detected. As mentioned above, this argues for cross-sectoral analyses of how policy making of all forms influences the texture and rhythm of daily life, and with what consequence for patterns of mobility or of energy consumption. There is, in addition, more to know about how the elements of practice circulate and about where responsibility lies for defining and facilitating conditions in which more sustainable ways of life might take hold.

What, then, are the chances that practice theory might capture recruits within the policy world? For the time being, policy relevant social science tends to be that which is consistent with a dominant paradigm organized around theories of individual attitude, behaviour and choice. At this point it is important to notice that policy makers' tastes in social theory are not entirely random. The ABC is a political and not just a theoretical position in that it locates both the problem and the response as a matter of individual behaviour. This view, which is in keeping with the idea that government's task is in essence that of encouraging citizens to adopt pro-environmental behaviours, down-plays the extent to which the state sustains unsustainable institutions, conventions and ways of life, and the extent to which it has a hand in structuring options and possibilities. This is awkward in that the chances of embedding a more practice–theoretical approach depend on highlighting and exploiting rather than obscuring these roles.

Like other practices, styles of governance have trajectories and careers of their own. As we have shown, climate change policy making is not of a piece and is in any case only part of the picture: it may not happen any time soon, but it is possible to imagine future transitions in how proc-esses of social change are conceptualized, resulting in a rush of policy interest in what theories of practice have to offer.

REFERENCES

Abernathy, W. and K. Clark (1985) 'Innovation – mapping the winds of creative destruction.' *Research Policy*, 14(1): 3–22.

Agate, E. (2005) *Woodlands: A practical handbook*. Doncaster: BTCV.

Ajzen, I. (1991) 'The theory of planned behavior.' *Organizational Behavior and Human Decision Processes*, 50(2): 179–211.

Akrich, M. (1992) 'The de-scription of technical objects.' In W. Bijker and J. Law (eds) *Shaping Technology/Building Society*. Cambridge, MA: MIT Press.

Amin, A. and N. Thrift (2007) 'Cultural-economy and cities.' *Progress in Human Geography*, 31(2): 143–161.

Appadurai, A. (1986) *The Social Life of Things: Commodities in cultural perspective*. Cambridge: Cambridge University Press.

Armstrong, D. (1983) *Political Anatomy of the Body: Medical knowledge in Britain in the twentieth century*. Cambridge: Cambridge University Press.

Armstrong, D. (1995) 'The rise of surveillance medicine.' *Sociology of Health & Illness*, 17(3): 393–404.

Becker, H. (1963) *Outsiders*. New York: The Free Press.

Becker, H. S. (1977) *Boys in White: Student culture in medical school*. New Brunswick and London: Transaction.

Berkhout, F., A. Smith and A. Stirling (2004) 'Socio-technological regimes and transition contexts.' In B. Elzen, F. W. Geels and K. Green (eds) *System Innovation and the Transition to Sustainability: Theory, evidence and policy*. Cheltenham: Edward Elgar: 48–75.

Blair, T. (2006) *Climate Change: The UK programme*. London: HMSO.

Boero, N. (2007) 'All the news that's fat to print: the American "obesity epidemic" and the media.' *Qualitative Sociology*, 30(1): 41–60.

Borden, I. (2001) *Skateboarding and the City*. Oxford: Berg.

Borg, K. (1999) 'The "chauffeur problem" in the early auto era: structuration theory and the users of technology.' *Technology and Culture*, 40(4): 797–832.

Borg, K. (2007) *Auto Mechanics: Technology and expertise in twentieth-century America*. Baltimore, MD: Johns Hopkins University Press.

Bourdieu, P. (1977) *Outline of a Theory of Practice*. (1972) Trans. Richard Nice. Cambridge: Cambridge University Press.

Bourdieu, P. (1984) *Distinction: A social critique of judgement and taste*. London: Routledge.

Bourdieu, P. (1990) *The Logic of Practice*. Stanford: Stanford University Press.

Bowker, G. and S. Star (2000a) *Sorting Things Out: Classification and its consequences*. Cambridge, MA: MIT Press.

Bowker, G. C. and S. L. Star (2000b) 'Invisible mediators of action: classification and the ubiquity of standards.' *Mind, Culture & Activity* 7: 147–163.

Branca, F., H. Nikogosian and T. Lobstein (2007) *The Challenge of Obesity in the WHO European Region and Strategies for Response*. Copenhagen: World Health Organization Regional Office for Europe.

Brangwyn, B. and R. Hopkins (2008) *Transition Initiatives Primer*. Vancouver: First Nations Technology Council. Accessed 28.07.11 at http://fnbc.info/content/guide-transition-initiatives-primer-ben-brangwyn-and-rob-hopkins.

Brown, J. S. and P. Duguid (2001) 'Knowledge and organization: a social-practice perspective.' *Organization Science*, 12(2): 198–213.

Burke, T. (1996) *Lifebuoy Men, Lux Women: Commodification, consumption and cleanliness in modern Zimbabwe*. London: Leicester University Press.

Cabinet Office Strategy Unit (2009) *An Analysis of Urban Transport*. London: HMSO.

Cain, C. (1991) 'Personal stories: identity acquisition and self-understanding in Alcoholics Anonymous.' *Ethos*, 19(2): 210–253.

Callaway, H. (1992) 'Dressing for dinner in the bush: rituals of self-definition and British imperial authority.' In R. Barnes and J. Eicher (eds) *Dress and Gender: Making and meaning in cultural contexts.* Oxford: Berg.

Cieraad, I. (2002) '"Out of my kitchen!" Architecture, gender and domestic efficiency.' *The Journal of Architecture,* 7(3): 263–279.

Cohen, S. (1987) *Folk Devils and Moral Panics: The creation of the mods and rockers.* Oxford: Blackwell.

Cowan, R. S. (1983) *More Work for Mother: The ironies of household technology from the open hearth to the microwave.* New York: Basic Books.

Crossley, N. (2006) 'In the gym: motives, meaning and moral careers.' *Body and Society,* 12(3): 23–50.

Crossley, N. (2008) 'Pretty connected: the social network of the early UK punk movement.' *Theory, Culture and Society,* 25(6): 89–116.

D'Adderio, L. (2008) 'The performativity of routines: theorising the influence of artefacts and distributed agencies on routines dynamics.' *Research Policy,* 37: 769–789.

Dahrendorf, R. (1979) *Life Chances: Approaches to social and political theory.* Chicago: Chicago University Press.

Dant, T. (2010) 'The work of repair: gesture, emotion and sensual knowledge.' *Sociological Research Online,* 15(3): 7.

Darnton, A. (2010) EVO502: Unlocking Habits/Reconfiguring Routines: Final Report to DEFRA.

DCMS/Strategy Unit (2002) *Game Plan: A strategy for delivering government's sport and physical activity objectives.* London: Cabinet Office.

De Dear, R. J. (2007) 'Comments on "Clothing as a mobile environment for human beings – prospects of clothing for the future" presented by Teruko Tamura, Presidential Address to ICHES'05 Tokyo, Japan 12–15 September 2005.' *Journal of the Human-Environmental System,* 10(1): 45–46.

de la Bruheze, A. (2000) 'Bicycle use in twentieth century Western Europe: the comparison of nine cities.' Accessed 28.07.11 at www.velomondial.net/velomondiall2000/PDF/BRUHEZE.PDF.

De Wit, O., J. Van den Ende, J. Schot and E. Van Oost (2002) 'Innovation junctions – office technologies in the Netherlands, 1880–1980.' *Technology and Culture,* 43(1): 50–72.

DEFRA (2008) *A Framework for Pro-environmental Behaviours.* London: HMSO.

Deuten, J. (2003) *Cosmopolitanising Technologies.* PhD dissertation, University of Twente, Enschede.

Disco, C. and B. van der Meulen (eds) (1998) *Getting New Technologies Together: Studies in making sociotechnical order.* Berlin: de Gruyter.

Donzelot, J. and R. Hurley (1980) *The Policing of Families.* London: Hutchinson.

Douglas, M. (1984) *Purity and Danger: An analysis of the concepts of pollution and taboo.* London: Routledge.

Duguid, P. (2005) '"The art of knowing": social and tacit dimensions of knowledge and the limits of the community of practice.' *Information Society*, 21: 109–118.

Edensor, T. (2004) 'Automobility and national identity.' *Theory, Culture and Society*, 21(4–5): 101–120.

Elias, N. (1969) *The Civilizing Process: The history of manners and state formation and civilization.* Oxford: Blackwell.

Elias, N. (1995) 'Technicization and civilization.' *Theory, Culture and Society*, 12(3): 7–42.

Ellis, A. (1969) *All About Home Freezing.* London: Hamlyn.

Ellis, A. (1976) *Easy Freeze Cooking.* London: Corgi.

Ellis, A. (1978) *Hamlyn All Colour Freezer Cook Book.* London: Hamlyn.

Elzen, B., F. W. Geels and K. Green (eds) (2004) *System Innovation and the Transition to Sustainability: Theory, evidence and policy.* Cheltenham: Edward Elgar.

Evans, B. (2006) '"Gluttony or Sloth": critical geographies of bodies and morality in (anti)obesity policy.' *Area*, 38: 259–267.

Fanger, P. O. (1973) 'Assessment of man's thermal comfort in practice.' *British Journal of Industrial Medicine*, 30(4): 313–324.

Franke, N. and S. Shah (2003) 'How communities support innovative activities: an exploration of assistance and sharing among end-users.' *Research Policy*, 32(1): 157–178.

Frederick, C. (1920) *Scientific Management in the Home: Household engineering.* Chicago, IL: American School of Home Economics.

Gagge, A., H. Burton and C. Bazett (1941) 'A practical system of units for the description of the heat exchange of man with his environment.' *Science* 94(2445): 428–430.

Gagnon, J. H. and W. Simon (1974) *Sexual Conduct: The social sources of human sexuality*. London: Hutchinson.

Garnett, T. and T. Jackson (2007) 'Frost bitten: an exploration of refrigeration dependence in the UK food chain and its implications for climate policy.' Paper presented at the 11th European Round Table on Sustainable Consumption and Production, Basel, Switzerland.

Gartman, D. (1994) *Auto Opium: A social history of American automobile design*. London: Routledge.

Gartman, D. (2004) 'Three ages of the automobile.' *Theory, Culture and Society*, 21(4–5): 169–195.

Garvey, P. (2001) 'Driving, drinking and daring in Norway.' In D. Miller (ed.) *Car Cultures*. Oxford: Berg: 133–153.

Gatersleben, B. and C. Vlek (1998) 'Household consumption, quality of life and environmental impacts.' In T. Noorman and T. Schoot-Uiterkamp (eds) *Green Households?* London: Earthscan: 141–183.

Geddes, P. (1915) *Cities in Evolution*. London: Williams and Norgate.

Geels, F. W. (2002) *Understanding the Dynamics of Technological Transitions: A co-evolutionary and socio-technical analysis*. Enschede: Twente University Press.

Geels, F. W. (2004) 'From sectoral systems of innovation to socio-technical systems: insights about dynamics and change from sociology and institutional theory.' *Research Policy*, 33(6–7): 897–920.

Geels, F. W. (2005) *Technological Transitions and System Innovations: A co-evolutionary and socio-technical analysis*. Cheltenham: Edward Elgar.

Geels, F. W. and J. Schot (2007) 'Typology of sociotechnical transition pathways.' *Research Policy*, 36: 399–417.

Geels, F. W. and J. Schot (2010) 'Part 1: The dynamics of socio-technical transitions: a socio-technical perspective.' In J. Grin, J. Rotmans and J. Schot (eds) *Transitions to Sustainable Development: New Directions in the study of long term transformative change*. London: Routledge: 11–104.

Giddens, A. (1984) *The Constitution of Society*. Cambridge: Polity Press.

Gilbreth, L. (1927) *The Home-maker and Her Job*. New York: Appleton.

Goffman, E. (1975 [1961]) *Asylums: Essays on the social situation of mental patients and other inmates*. Harmondsworth: Penguin.

Graham, S. and S. Marvin (2001) *Splintering Urbanism: Networked infrastructures, technological mobilities and the urban condition*. London: Routledge.

Gregson, N. (2007) *Living With Things: Ridding, accommodation, dwelling*. Wantage: Sean Kingston.

Griffith, G. and J. Holden (2004) 'The way we live now: daily life in the 21st century.' *Market Research Society*. Accessed 28.07.11 at http:// bbcdailylife.tns-global.com/.

Grin, J., J. Rotmans and J. Schot (2010) 'Introduction: from persistent problems to system innovations and transitions?' In J. Grin, J. Rotmans and J. Schot (eds) *Transitions to Sustainable Development: New directions in the study of long term transformative change*. London: Routledge: 1–10.

Gronow, J. (2009) 'Fads, fashions and "real" innovations: novelties and social change.' In E. Shove, F. Trentmann and R. Wilk (eds) *Time, Consumption and Everyday Life*. Oxford: Berg: 129–143.

Hand, M. and E. Shove (2007) 'Condensing practices: ways of living with a freezer.' *Journal of Consumer Culture*, 7(1): 79–104.

Hand, M., E. Shove and D. Southerton (2005) 'Explaining showering: a discussion of the material, conventional, and temporal dimensions of practice.' *Sociological Research Online*, 10(2).

Harris, H. (2008) 'Conquering winter: U.S. consumers and the cast-iron stove.' *Building Research and Information*, 36(4): 337–350.

Harrison, P. (2009) 'In the absence of practice.' *Environment and Planning Development: Society and Space*, 17(6): 987–1009.

Hebdige, D. (1979) *Subculture: The meaning of style*. London: Methuen.

Hebdige, D. (1988) *Hiding in the Light: On images and things*. London: Comedia.

Heidegger, M. (1962) *Being and Time*. Trans. J. Macquarrie and E. Robinson. Oxford: Blackwell.

Hertzen, H. v. and P. D. Spreiregen (1971) *Building a New Town: Finland's new garden city, Tapiola*. Cambridge, MA: MIT Press.

Hess, M. (2006) 'It's a family affair: the media evolution of global families in a digital age.' New York: OMD. Accessed 28.07.11 at http://l.yimg.com/au.yimg.com/i/pr/familyaffair_final.pdf.

Hochschild, A. (2001) *The Time Bind: When work becomes home and home becomes work.* New York: Henry Holt.

House of Commons Health Committee (2004) *Obesity: Volume 1.* London: The Stationery Office.

House of Lords Science and Technology Select Committee (2010) 'Call for Evidence: Behaviour Change – Travel-Mode Choice Interventions to Reduce Car Use in Towns and Cities.' Accessed 28.07.11 at www. parliament.uk/documents/lords-committees/science-technology/behaviourchange/CfEBCtravelmodechoice.pdf.

Howard, E., L. Mumford and F. J. S. Osborn (1951) *Garden Cities of Tomorrow.* London: Faber.

Hughes, T. (1993 [1983]) *Networks of Power: Electrification in Western society, 1880–1930.* Baltimore, MD: Johns Hopkins University Press.

Hui, A. (2011) *Enthusiastic Travel: Theorizing processes and mobilities of practices in leisure careers.* PhD dissertation, Sociology Department, Lancaster University.

Humphreys, D. (2003) 'Selling out snowboarding: the alternative response to commercial co-optation.' In R. Reinhart and S. Sydnor (eds) *To The Extreme: Alternative sports.* Albany, NY: SUNY Press: 407–429.

Hutchins, E. (1993) 'Learning to navigate'. In S. Chaiklin and J. Lave (eds) *Understanding Practice.* Cambridge, MA: Cambridge University Press: 35–64.

Hutchins, E. B. (1995) *Cognition in the Wild.* Cambridge, MA: MIT Press.

Ingold, T. (2008) 'When ANT meets SPIDER: social theory for arthropods.' In C. Knappett and I. Malafouris (eds) *Material Agency.* New York: Springer: 209–217.

Institute for Government (2009) Mindspace: influencing behaviour through public policy. Accessed 28.07.11 at http://www.instituteforgovernment.org.uk/publications_download.php?id=2

Isaac, M. and D. P. van Vuuren (2009) 'Modeling global residential sector energy demand for heating and air conditioning in the context of climate change.' *Energy Policy,* 37(2): 507–521.

Ito, M. and B. Okabe (2005) 'Technosocial situations: emergent structuring of mobile e-mail use.' In M. Ito, B. Okabe and M. Matsuda (eds) *Personal, Portable, Pedestrian: Mobile phones in Japanese life.* Cambridge, MA: MIT Press.

Jerram, L. (2006) 'Kitchen sink dramas: women, modernity and space in Weimar Germany.' *Cultural Geographies,* 13: 538–556.

Jones, R., J. Pykett and M. Whitehead (2010) 'Governing temptation: changing behaviour in an age of libertarian paternalism.' *Progress in Human Geography*: 1–19.

Kaufmann, J.-C. (1998) *Dirty Linen: Couples and their laundry.* London: Middlesex University Press.

Kemp, R., A. Rip and J. Schot (2001) 'Constructing transition paths through the management of niches.' In R. Garud and P. Carnoe (eds) *Path Dependence and Creation.* Mahwah, NJ: Lawrence Erlbaum: 269–299.

Kline, R. and T. Pinch (1996) 'Users as agents of technological change: the social construction of the automobile in the rural United States.' *Technology and Culture,* 37(4): 763–795.

Knerr, R. (1997) 'Hula hoop.' Accessed 28.07.11 at http://web.mit.edu/invent/iow/hulahoop.html.

Knorr Cetina, K. (1997) 'Sociality with objects.' *Theory, Culture and Society,* 14(4): 1–30.

Knorr Cetina, K. (2003) 'From pipes to scopes: the flow architecture of financial markets.' *Distinktion,* (7): 7–23.

Knorr Cetina, K. (2005a) 'Complex global microstructures.' *Theory, Culture and Society,* 22(5): 213–234.

Knorr Cetina, K. (2005b) 'How are global markets global? The architecture of a flow world.' In K. Knorr-Cetina and A. Preda (eds) *The Sociology of Financial Markets.* Oxford: Oxford University Press: 38–61.

Knorr Cetina, K. and U. Bruegger (2000) 'The market as an object of attachment: exploring postsocial relations in financial markets.' *Canadian Journal of Sociology,* 25(2): 141–168.

Knorr Cetina, K. and A. Preda (2007) 'The temporalization of financial markets: from network markets to flow markets.' *Theory, Culture and Society,* 24(7–8): 123–145.

Kraut, R., M. Patterson, V. Lundmark, S. Kiesler, T. Mukophadhyay and W. Scherlis (1998) 'Internet paradox: a social technology that reduces social involvement and psychological well-being?' *American Psychologist*, 53(9): 1017–1031.

Kreitzman, L. (1999) *The 24 Hour Society*. London: Profile.

Kuhn, T. (1970) *The structure of scientific revolutions*. Chicago, IL: University of Chicago Press.

Larsen, J., K. W. Axhausen and J. Urry (2006) 'Geographies of social networks: meetings, travel and communications.' *Mobilities*, 1(2): 261–283.

Latour, B. (1987) *Science In Action: How to follow scientists and engineers through society*. Cambridge, MA: Harvard University Press.

Latour, B. (1990) 'Visualization and cognition: drawing things together.' Accessed 28.07.11 at www.bruno-latour.fr/articles/article/21-DRAWING-THINGS-TOGETHER.pdf.

Latour, B. (2000) 'When things strike back: a possible contribution of "science studies" to the social sciences.' *British Journal of Sociology*, 51(1): 107–125.

Latour, B. and S. Woolgar (1986) *Laboratory Life: The construction of scientific facts*. Princeton, NJ: Princeton University Press.

Laurier, E. (2001) 'Why people say where they are during mobile phone calls.' *Environment and Planning Development: Society and Space*, 19(4): 485–504.

Lave, J. and E. Wenger (1991) *Situated Learning: Legitimate peripheral participation*. Cambridge: Cambridge University Press.

Law, J. (1986) 'On the methods of long distance control: vessels, navigation, and the Portuguese route to India.' In J. Law (ed.) *Power, Action and Belief: A new sociology of knowledge?* Oxford: Routledge: 234–263.

Law, J. (1987) 'Technology and heterogeneous engineering: the Case of Portuguese expansion.' In W. Bijker and T. Pinch (eds) *The Social Construction of Technological Systems: New directions in the sociology and history of technology*. Cambridge, MA: MIT Press: 111–134.

Law, J. (1991) *A Sociology of Monsters: Essays on power, technology and domination*. London: Routledge.

Law, J. (1992) Notes on the theory of the actor-network: ordering, strategy, and heterogeneity. 'Systemic Practice and Action Research, 5: 379–393.

Lefebvre, H. (2004) Rhythm Analysis: Space, time, and everyday life. London: Continuum.

Ling, R. and B. Yttri (2002) 'Hypercoordination via mobile phones in Norway.' In J. Katz and M. Aakhus (eds) Perpetual Contact: Mobile communication, private talk, public performance. Cambridge: Cambridge University Press: 139–170.

Lizardo, O. (2009) 'Is a "special psychology" of practice possible? From values and attitudes to embodied dispositions.' Theory and Psychology, 19: 1–15.

Lizardo, O. and M. Strand (2010) 'Skills, toolkits, contexts and institutions: clarifying the relationship between different approaches to cognition in cultural sociology.' Poetics, 38: 204–227.

Loorbach, D. and J. Rotmans (2010) 'Towards a better understanding of transitions and their governance: a systemic and reflexive approach.' In J. Grin, J. Rotmans and J. Schot (eds) Transitions to Sustainable Development: new directions in the study of long term transformative change. London: Routledge.

Lury, C. (2004) Brands: The logos of the global economy. London: Routledge.

MacAndrew, C. and R. B. Edgerton (1969) Drunken Comportment: A social explanation. Chicago, IL: Aldine.

MacIntyre, A. (1985) After Virtue. London: Duckworth.

Mail online (2005) 'History of the humble driving test.' Accessed 20.07.11 at www.dailymail.co.uk/news/article-341091/History-humble-driving-test.html.

Manzini, E. and P. Cau (1989) The Material of Invention. Cambridge, MA: MIT Press.

McCracken, G. (1988) Culture and Consumption: New approaches to the symbolic character of consumer goods and activities. Bloomington, IN: Indiana University Press.

McNeil, P. and V. Karaminas (eds) (2009) The Men's Fashion Reader. Oxford: Berg.

Melosi, M. (2000) The Sanitary City: Urban infrastructure in America from colonial times to the present. Baltimore, MD: Johns Hopkins University Press.

Merriman, P. (2006) '"Mirror, signal, manoeuvre": assembling and governing the motorway driver in late 1950s Britain.' *Sociological Review*, 54: 75–92.

Meyersohn, R. and E. Katz (1957) 'Notes on a natural history of fads.' *The American Journal of Sociology*, 62(6): 594–601.

Miettinen, R. and J. Virkkunen (2005) 'Epistemic objects, artefacts and organizational change.' *Organization*, 12(3): 437–456.

Miller, D. (2001) 'Driven societies.' In D. Miller (ed.) *Car Cultures*. Oxford: Berg: 1–33.

Miller, P. and N. S. Rose (2008) *Governing the Present: Administering economic, social and personal life*. Cambridge: Polity Press.

Molotch, H. (2003) *Where Stuff Comes From: How toasters, toilets, cars, computers, and many others things come to be as they are*. London: Routledge.

Mumford, L. (1939) *The City in History: Its origins, its transformations, and its prospects*. New York: Harcourt, Brace and World.

Muthesius, S. (1982) *The English Terraced House*. New Haven, CT: Yale University Press.

Nie, N. H. (2001) 'Sociability, interpersonal relations, and the Internet: reconciling conflicting findings.' *American Behavioral Scientist*, 45(3): 420–435.

O'Dell, T. (2001) 'Raggare and the panic of mobility: modernity and hybridity in Sweden.' In D. Miller (ed.) *Car Cultures*. Oxford: Berg: 105–132.

O'Neill, B. (2010) 'A message to the illiberal nudge industry: push off.' Accessed 28.07.11 at www.spiked-online.com/index.php/site/article/9840/.

Ogle, M. (1996) *All the Modern Conveniences: American household plumbing, 1840–1890*. Baltimore, MD: Johns Hopkins University Press.

Orlikowski, W. J. (2002) 'Knowing in practice: enacting a collective capability in distributed organizing.' *Organization Science*, 13(3): 249–273.

Oudshoorn, N. and T. J. Pinch (2005) *How Users Matter: The co-construction of users and technology*. Cambridge, MA: MIT.

Pantzar, M. and R. Sundell-Nieminen (2003) 'Towards an ecology of goods: symbiosis and competition between household goods.' In

I. Koskinen (ed.) *Empathic Design: User experience in product design.* Helsinki: IT Press.

Parr, J. (1999) *Domestic Goods: The material, the moral, and the economic in the postwar years.* Toronto: University of Toronto Press.

Philp, R. (1856) *Enquire within Upon Everything: The great Victorian standby.* London: Houlston and Stoneman.

Pickering, A. (1995) *The Mangle of Practice: Time, agency, and science.* Chicago, IL: University of Chicago Press.

Pooley, C. and J. Turnbull (2000) 'Modal choice and modal change: the journey to work in Britain since 1890.' *Journal of Transport Geography*, 8: 11–24.

Pred, A. (1981) 'Social reproduction and the time-geography of everyday life.' *Geografiska Annaler. Series B. Human Geography*, 63(1): 5–22.

Preda, A. (1999) 'The turn to things: arguments for a sociological theory of things.' *Sociological Quarterly*, 40(4): 347–366.

Preda, A. (2009) *Framing Finance.* Chicago, IL: Chicago University Press.

Prendergast, J., B. Foley, V. Menne and A. K. Isaac (2008) *Creatures of Habit? The art of behavioural change.* London: The Social Market Foundation.

Pucher, J. and R. Buehler (2008) 'Making cycling irresistable: lessons from the Netherlands, Denmark and Germany.' *Transport Reviews*, 28(4): 495–528.

Reckwitz, A. (2002) 'Toward a theory of social practices: a development in culturalist theorizing.' *European Journal of Social Theory*, 5(2): 243–263.

Rip, A. (1998) 'Modern and postmodern science policy.' *EASST Review.* Accessed 28.07.11. at www.easst.net/review/sept1998/rip.shtml.

Rip, A. (2006) 'A co-evolutionary approach to reflexive governance and its ironies.' In J. P. Voβ, D. Bauknecht and R. Kemp (eds) *Reflexive Governance for Sustainable Development.* Cheltenham: Edward Elgar: 82–100.

Rip, A. and R. Kemp (1998) 'Technological change.' In S. Rayner and E. Malone (eds) *Human Choices and Climate Change.* Columbus, OH: Battelle: 327–399.

Røpke, I. (2001) 'New technology in everyday life – social processes and environmental impact.' *Ecological Economics*, 38(3): 403–422.

Røpke, I. (2009) 'Theories of practice – new inspiration for ecological economic studies on consumption.' *Ecological Economics*, 68(10): 2490–2497.

Rotmans, J., R. Kemp and M. Van Asselt (2001) 'More evolution than revolution: transition management in public policy.' *Foresight – The journal of future studies, strategic thinking and policy*, 3: 15–31.

Ruibal, S. (2006) 'Halfpipe judges bend a bit as sport evolves.' Accessed 12.07.08 at www.usatoday.com/sports/olympics/torino/snowboarding/2006–02–09-halfpipe-judging_x.htm.

Sachs, W. and D. Reneau (1992) *For Love of the Automobile: Looking back into the history of our desires*. Berkeley, CA: University of California Press.

Schatzki, T. (1996) *Social Practices: A Wittgensteinian approach to human activity and the social*. Cambridge: Cambridge University Press.

Schatzki, T. (2002) *The Site of the Social: A philosophical account of the constitution of social life and change*. University Park, PA: Pennsylvania State University Press.

Schatzki, T. (2010a) 'Materiality and social life.' *Nature and Culture*, 5(2): 123–149.

Schatzki, T. (2010b) *Timespace and Human Activity*. Lanham, MD: Lexington Books.

Schatzki, T., K. Knorr-Cetina and E. von Savigny (eds) (2001) *The Practice Turn in Contemporary Theory*. London: Routledge.

Schor, J. B. (1991) *The Overworked American: The unexpected decline of leisure*. New York: Basic Books.

Sheller, M. and J. Urry (2000) 'The city and the car.' *International Journal of Urban and Regional Research*, 24: 737–757.

Shove, E. (2003) *Comfort, Cleanliness and Convenience: The social organization of normality*. Oxford: Berg.

Shove, E. (2009) 'Everyday practice and the production and consumption of time.' In E. Shove, F. Trentmann and R. Wilk (eds) *Time, Consumption and Everyday Life: Practice, materiality and culture*. Oxford: Berg: 17–35.

Shove, E. (2010) 'Beyond the ABC: climate change policy and theories of social change.' *Environment and Planning A*, 42(6): 1273–1285.

Shove, E. and M. Pantzar (2005) 'Consumers, producers and practices: understanding the invention and reinvention of Nordic Walking.' *Journal of Consumer Culture*, 5(1): 43–64.

Shove, E. and M. Pantzar (2006) 'Fossilisation.' *Ethnologia Europaea: Journal of European Ethnology*, 35(1–2): 59–63.

Shove, E. and D. Southerton (2000) 'Defrosting the freezer: from novelty to convenience (a narrative of normalization).' *Journal of Material Culture*, 5(3): 301–319.

Shove, E. and G. Walker (2007) 'CAUTION! Transitions ahead: politics, practice, and sustainable transition management.' *Environment and Planning A*, 39(4): 763–770.

Shove, E., M. Watson, M. Hand and J. Ingram (2007) *The Design of Everyday Life*. Oxford: Berg.

Siegelbaum, L. H. (2008) *Cars for Comrades: The life of the Soviet automobile*. Ithaca, NY: Cornell University Press.

Silverstone, R. (1993) 'Time, information and communication technologies and the household.' *Time and Society*, 2(3): 283–311.

Simmel, G. (1957) 'Fashion.' *The American Journal of Sociology*, 62(6): 541–558.

Simmel, G. (2002) 'The metropolis and mental life.' In T. Bennett and D. Watson (eds) *Understanding Everyday Life*. Oxford: Blackwell: 124–126.

Sivak, M. (2009) 'Potential energy demand for cooling in the 50 largest metropolitan areas of the world: implications for developing countries.' *Energy Policy*, 37(4): 1382–1384.

Slade, T. (2009) 'The Japanese suit and modernity.' In P. McNeil and V. Karaminas (eds) *The Men's Fashion Reader*. Oxford: Berg: 289–298.

Slater, D. (2003) 'Modernity under construction: building the Internet in Trinidad.' In P. Brey, T. Misa and A. Feenberg (eds) *Modernity and Technology*. Cambridge, MA: MIT Press: 19–160.

Smith, A., A. Stirling and F. Berkhout (2005) 'The governance of sustainable socio-technical transitions.' *Research Policy*, 34(10): 1491–1510.

Southerton, D. (2003) '"Squeezing time" – allocating practices, coordinating networks and scheduling society.' *Time and Society*, 12(1): 5–25.

Southerton, D. (2006) 'Analysing the temporal organization of daily life.' *Sociology*, 40(3): 435–454.

Spradley, J. P. and B. J. Mann (1975) *Cocktail Waitress: Woman's work in a man's world*. New York: McGraw Hill.

Strasser, S. (1999) *Waste and Want: A social history of trash*. New York: Metropolitan Books.

Suchman, L. A. (1984) *Plans and Situated Actions: An inquiry into the idea of human-machine communication*. Berkeley, CA: University of California.

Suchman, L., J. Blomberg, J. Orr and R. Trigg (1999) 'Reconstructing technologies as social practice.' *American Behavioral Scientist*, 43(3): 392–408.

Sudnow, D. (1993) *Ways of the Hand: The organization of improvised conduct*. Cambridge, MA: MIT Press.

Sustainable Consumption Round Table (2006) 'I will if you will.' Accessed 28.07.11 at www.sd-commission.org.uk/publications/downloads/I_Will_If_You_Will.pdf.

Sustrans (2008) 'Why cycle?' Accessed 28.07.11 at www.sustrans.org.uk/assets/files/leaflets/sustrans_whycycle_March08.pdf.

Taylor, C. (1971) 'Interpretation and the sciences of man.' *The Review of Metaphysics*, 25(1): 3–51.

Team-6 Committee and Ministry of the Environment (Japan) (2007) *Cool Biz/Warm Biz*. Accessed 28.07.11 at www.team-6.jp/english/result.html.

Thaler, R. H. and C. R. Sunstein (2009) *Nudge: Improving decisions about health, wealth and happiness*. London: Penguin.

The Scottish Government (2008) *Scottish Sustainable Communities Initiative*. Accessed 28.07.11 at www.scotland.gov.uk/Publications/2008/06/25093645/16.

Thompson, C. (1996) 'Caring consumers: gendered consumption meanings and the juggling lifestyle.' *Journal of Consumer Research*, 22: 388–407.

Thompson, E. P. (1967) 'Time, work-discipline, and industrial capital.' *Past and Present*, 38: 56–97.

Thorpe, H. (2005) 'Jibbing the gender order: females in the snowboarding culture.' *Sport in Society*, 8(1): 76–100.

Thrift, N. (2004) 'Driving in the city.' *Theory, Culture and Society*,
21(4–5): 41.

Times online (2008) 'Ian Hibell, cyclist who pedalled world, killed by
hit-and-run driver.' Accessed 28.07.11 at www.timesonline.co.uk/tol/
news/uk/article4673693.ece.

Turner, S. (2001) 'Throwing out the tacit rule book: learning and practices.' In T. Schatzki, K. Knorr-Cetina and E. Von Savigny (eds) *The
Practice Turn in Social Theory*. London: Routledge: 120–131.

Tushman, M. L. and P. Anderson (1986) 'Technological discontinuities
and organizational environments.' *Administrative Science Quarterly*,
31(3): 439–465.

UK Cabinet Office (2010) 'The coalition: our programme for government. Accessed 29.11.11 at www.cabinetoffice.gov.uk/news/coaltion-
documents.

United Nations Environment Programme (2008) 'Kick the habit: a UN
guide to climate change neutrality.' Accessed 28.07.11 at www.unep.
org/publications/ebooks/kick-the-habit/.

Urry, J. (2004) 'The "System" of Automobility.' *Theory, Culture and
Society*, 21(4–5): 25–39.

Urry, J. (2006) 'Inhabiting the car.' *Sociological Review*, 54: 17–31.

Urry, J. (2007) *Mobilities*. Cambridge: Polity Press.

Volti, R. (1996) 'A century of automobility.' *Technology and Culture*,
37(4): 663–685.

Voβ, J.-P., R. Kemp and D. Bauknecht (2006) *Reflexive Governance for
Sustainable Development*. Cheltenham: Edward Elgar.

Walker, G. (2009) *The Water and Energy Implications of Bathing and
Showering Behaviours and Technologies*. London: Waterwise.

Wang, S. (2007) *Becoming Taiwanese: Everyday practices and identity
transformation*. PhD dissertation, Sociology Department, Lancaster
University.

Warde, A. (2005) 'Consumption and theories of practice.' *Journal of
Consumer Culture*, 5(2): 131–153.

Warr, A. (2000) *Roofing Corrugated Iron – options for repair*. Material
evidence: conserving the building fabric. Parramatta: NSW Heritage
Office.

Watson, M. and E. Shove (2008) 'Product, competence, project and practice.' *Journal of Consumer Culture*, 8(1): 69–89.

Weber, H. (2005) 'Portable pleasures.' In M. Pantzar and E. Shove (eds) *Manufacturing leisure*. Helsinki: National Consumer Research Centre: 134–159.

Wenger, E. (1999) *Communities of Practice: Learning, meaning, and identity*. Cambridge: Cambridge University Press.

Wenger, E. and W. Snyder (2000) 'Communities of practice: the organizational frontier.' *Harvard Business Review*, 78: 139–145.

Wilhite, H., H. Nakagami and C. Murakoshi (1997) 'Changing patterns of air conditioning consumption in Japan.' In P. Bertholdi, A. Ricci and E. Wajer (eds) *Energy Efficiency in Household Appliances*. Berlin: Springer: 149–158.

Wolf, W. (1996) *Car Mania: A critical history of modern transport, 1770–1990*. London: Pluto.

World Standards (2011) 'Why do some countries drive on the right and others on the left?' Accessed 28.07.11 at http://users.telenet.be/worldstandards/driving%20on%20the%20left.htm#history.

Young, D. (2001) 'The life and death of cars: private vehicles on the Pitjantjatjara Lands, South Australia.' In D. Miller (ed.) *Car Cultures*. Oxford: Berg: 35–57.

Zerubavel, E. (1979) *Patterns of Time in Hospital Life: a sociological perspective*. Chicago, IL: University of Chicago Press.

Zerubavel, E. (1982) 'The standardization of time: a sociohistorical perspective.' *The American Journal of Sociology*, 88(1): 1–23.

Zwick, D. and N. Dholakia (2006) 'The epistemic consumption object and postsocial consumption: expanding consumer-object theory in consumer research.' *Consumption, Markets and Culture*, 9(1): 17–43.

INDEX